Practice*Planners*

Arthur E. Jongsma, Jr., Series Editor

Helping therapists help their clients…

Treatment Planners cover all the necessary elements for developing formal treatment plans, including detailed problem definitions, long-term goals, short-term objectives, therapeutic interventions, and DSM™ diagnoses.

Over 1,000,000 Practice *Planners* sold

WILEY

Practice*Planners*®

Homework Planners feature dozens of behaviorally based, ready-to-use assignments that are designed for use between sessions, as well as a CD-ROM (Microsoft Word) containing all of the assignments—allowing you to customize them to suit your unique client needs.

Progress Notes Planners contain complete prewritten progress notes for each presenting problem in the companion Treatment Planners.

Client Education Handout Planners contain elegantly designed handouts that can be printed out from the enclosed CD-ROM and provide information on a wide range of psychological and emotional disorders and life skills issues. Use as patient literature, handouts at presentations, and aids for promoting your mental health practice.

The Sexual Abuse Victim and Sexual Offender Treatment Planner, with DSM-5 Updates

Practice*Planners*® Series

Treatment Planners
The Complete Adult Psychotherapy Treatment Planner, Fifth Edition
The Child Psychotherapy Treatment Planner, Fifth Edition
The Adolescent Psychotherapy Treatment Planner, Fifth Edition
The Addiction Treatment Planner, Fifth Edition
The Continuum of Care Treatment Planner
The Couples Psychotherapy Treatment Planner, with DSM-5 Updates, Second Edition
The Employee Assistance Treatment Planner
The Pastoral Counseling Treatment Planner
The Older Adult Psychotherapy Treatment Planner, with DSM-5 Updates, Second Edition
The Behavioral Medicine Treatment Planner
The Group Therapy Treatment Planner, with DSM-5 Updates, Second Edition
The Gay and Lesbian Psychotherapy Treatment Planner
The Family Therapy Treatment Planner, with DSM-5 Updates, Second Edition
The Severe and Persistent Mental Illness Treatment Planner, with DSM-5 Updates, Second Edition
The Mental Retardation and Developmental Disability Treatment Planner
The Social Work and Human Services Treatment Planner
The Crisis Counseling and Traumatic Events Treatment Planner, with DSM-5 Updates, Second Edition
The Personality Disorders Treatment Planner
The Rehabilitation Psychology Treatment Planner
The Special Education Treatment Planner
The Juvenile Justice and Residential Care Treatment Planner
The School Counseling and School Social Work Treatment Planner, with DSM-5 Updates, Second Edition
The Sexual Abuse Victim and Sexual Offender Treatment Planner, with DSM-5 Updates
The Probation and Parole Treatment Planner
The Psychopharmacology Treatment Planner
The Speech-Language Pathology Treatment Planner
The Suicide and Homicide Risk Assessment and Prevention Treatment Planner, with DSM-5 Updates
The College Student Counseling Treatment Planner
The Parenting Skills Treatment Planner, with DSM-5 Updates
The Early Childhood Intervention Treatment Planner
The Co-occurring Disorders Treatment Planner, with DSM-5 Updates
The Complete Women's Psychotherapy Treatment Planner
The Veterans and Active Duty Military Psychotherapy Treatment Planner, with DSM-5 Updates

Progress Notes Planners
The Child Psychotherapy Progress Notes Planner, Fifth Edition
The Adolescent Psychotherapy Progress Notes Planner, Fifth Edition
The Adult Psychotherapy Progress Notes Planner, Fifth Edition
The Addiction Progress Notes Planner, Fifth Edition
The Severe and Persistent Mental Illness Progress Notes Planner, Second Edition
The Couples Psychotherapy Progress Notes Planner, Second Edition
The Family Therapy Progress Notes Planner, Second Edition
The Veterans and Active Duty Military Psychotherapy Progress Notes Planner

Homework Planners
Couples Therapy Homework Planner, Second Edition
Family Therapy Homework Planner, Second Edition
Grief Counseling Homework Planner
Group Therapy Homework Planner
Divorce Counseling Homework Planner
School Counseling and School Social Work Homework Planner, Second Edition
Child Therapy Activity and Homework Planner
Addiction Treatment Homework Planner, Fifth Edition
Adolescent Psychotherapy Homework Planner, Fifth Edition
Adult Psychotherapy Homework Planner, Fifth Edition
Child Psychotherapy Homework Planner, Fifth Edition
Parenting Skills Homework Planner
Veterans and Active Duty Military Psychotherapy Homework Planner

Client Education Handout Planners
Adult Client Education Handout Planner
Child and Adolescent Client Education Handout Planner
Couples and Family Client Education Handout Planner

Complete Planners
The Complete Depression Treatment and Homework Planner
The Complete Anxiety Treatment and Homework Planner

PracticePlanners®

Arthur E. Jongsma, Jr., Series Editor

The Sexual Abuse Victim and Sexual Offender Treatment Planner, with DSM-5 Updates

Rita Budrionis

Arthur E. Jongsma, Jr.

WILEY

Published by John Wiley & Sons, Inc., Hoboken, New Jersey.
Published simultaneously in Canada.

Limit of Liability/Disclaimer of Warranty: While the publisher and author have used their best efforts in preparing this book, they make no representations or warranties with respect to the accuracy or completeness of the contents of this book and specifically disclaim any implied warranties of merchantability or fitness for a particular purpose. No warranty may be created or extended by sales representatives or written sales materials. The advice and strategies contained herein may not be suitable for your situation. You should consult with a professional where appropriate. Neither the publisher nor author shall be liable for any loss of profit or any other commercial damages, including but not limited to special, incidental, consequential, or other damages.

This publication is designed to provide accurate and authoritative information in regard to the subject matter covered. It is sold with the understanding that the publisher is not engaged in rendering professional services. If legal, accounting, medical, psychological or any other expert assistance is required, the services of a competent professional person should be sought.

Designations used by companies to distinguish their products are often claimed as trademarks. In all instances where John Wiley & Sons, Inc. is aware of a claim, the product names appear in initial capital or all capital letters. Readers, however, should contact the appropriate companies for more complete information regarding trademarks and registration.

For general information on our other products and services please contact our Customer Care Department within the U.S. at (800) 762-2974, outside the United States at (317) 572-3993 or fax (317) 572-4002.

Wiley also publishes its books in a variety of electronic formats. Some content that appears in print may not be available in electronic books. For more information about Wiley products, please visit our website at www.wiley.com.

Library of Congress Cataloging-in-Publication Data:

ISBN 978-1-119-07332-1

Budrionis, Rita.
    The sexual abuse victim and sexual offender treatment planner, with DSM-5 updates / Rita Budrionis, Arthur E. Jongsma, Jr.
        p. cm. — (PracticePlanners series)
    ISBN 1-119-07332-4 (paper)
            1-119-07479-7 (ePDF)
            1-119-07481-9 (ePub)
    1. Sexual abuse victims—Handbooks, manuals, etc. 2. Sex crimes—Handbooks, manuals, etc. 3. Mental health services—Medical records—Handbooks, manuals, etc. I. Jongsma, Arthur E., 1943– II. Title. III. Practice planners.
    RC560.S44 B83 2003
    616.85′83—dc21
    2002014458

Printed in the United States of America

V10014258_092719

To Alfa, Bill, Christopher, Elizabeth, Mary, and Vito. You have all been my shining inspirations, my strong supporters, my gentle critics, and my patient teachers while sharing the joys of our family.

—*Rita Budrionis*

To Peggy Alexander, Cristina Wojdylo, and Judi Knott—a publication team that is unsurpassed in quality, dedication, creativity, and supportiveness.

—*Arthur E. Jongsma, Jr.*

CONTENTS

Practice*Planners*® Series Preface   xi
Acknowledgments   xiii
Introduction   1
Sample Treatment Plan   11

Part 1. VICTIM ISSUES

Anger Difficulties   15
Dissociation   23
Eating Disorders   31
Emotional Dysregulation   41
Posttraumatic Stress Disorder (PTSD)   50
Self-Blame   60
Self-Injury   69
Social Withdrawal   79
Trust Impairment   88

Part 2. OFFENDER ISSUES

Anger Difficulties   97
Cleric Offender   106
Cognitive Distortions   117
Denial   126
Deviant Sexual Arousal   137
Empathy Deficits   145
Female Offender   156
Guilt/Shame   164

Legal Issues   173
Relapse Prevention   182
Relationship Skills Deficits   191

Part 3.   OFFENDER AND VICTIM ISSUES

Anxiety, Panic, and Depression   203
Family Reunification   212
Self-Esteem Deficit   223
Sexual Dysfunction   231
Stress Management Deficits   241
Substance Abuse   249
Suicidal Ideation/Attempt   258

Appendix A: Bibliotherapy Suggestions   267
Appendix B: Recovery Model Objectives and Interventions   279

PRACTICE*PLANNERS*® SERIES PREFACE

Accountability is an important dimension of the practice of psychotherapy. Treatment programs, public agencies, clinics, and practitioners must justify and document their treatment plans to outside review entities in order to be reimbursed for services. The books in the Practice*Planners*® series are designed to help practitioners fulfill these documentation requirements efficiently and professionally.

The Practice*Planners*® series includes a wide array of treatment planning books including not only the original *Complete Adult Psychotherapy Treatment Planner*, *Child Psychotherapy Treatment Planner*, and *Adolescent Psychotherapy Treatment Planner*, all now in their fifth editions, but also *Treatment Planners* targeted to specialty areas of practice, including:

- Addictions
- Co-occurring disorders
- Behavioral medicine
- College students
- Couples therapy
- Crisis counseling
- Early childhood education
- Employee assistance
- Family therapy
- Gays and lesbians
- Group therapy
- Juvenile justice and residential care
- Mental retardation and developmental disability
- Neuropsychology
- Older adults
- Parenting skills
- Pastoral counseling
- Personality disorders

- Probation and parole
- Psychopharmacology
- Rehabilitation psychology
- School counseling and school social work
- Severe and persistent mental illness
- Sexual abuse victims and offenders
- Social work and human services
- Special education
- Speech-language pathology
- Suicide and homicide risk assessment
- Veterans and active military duty
- Women's issues

In addition, there are three branches of companion books that can be used in conjunction with the *Treatment Planners*, or on their own:

- *Progress Notes Planners* provide a menu of progress statements that elaborate on the client's symptom presentation and the provider's therapeutic intervention. Each *Progress Notes Planner* statement is directly integrated with the behavioral definitions and therapeutic interventions from its companion *Treatment Planner*.
- *Homework Planners* include homework assignments designed around each presenting problem (such as anxiety, depression, substance use, anger control problems, eating disorders, or panic disorder) that is the focus of a chapter in its corresponding *Treatment Planner*.
- *Client Education Handout Planners* provide brochures and handouts to help educate and inform clients on presenting problems and mental health issues, as well as life skills techniques. The handouts are included on CD-ROMs for easy printing from your computer and are ideal for use in waiting rooms, at presentations, as newsletters, or as information for clients struggling with mental illness issues. The topics covered by these handouts correspond to the presenting problems in the *Treatment Planners*.

The series also includes adjunctive books, such as *The Psychotherapy Documentation Primer* and *The Clinical Documentation Sourcebook*, contain forms and resources to aid the clinician in mental health practice management.

The goal of our series is to provide practitioners with the resources they need in order to provide high-quality care in the era of accountability. To put it simply: We seek to help you spend more time on patients, and less time on paperwork.

ARTHUR E. JONGSMA, JR.
Grand Rapids, Michigan

ACKNOWLEDGMENTS

First, I would like to thank Art Jongsma as the originator of this truly valuable series of Practice*Planners* books. Before working on this project, I frequently used his books to assist with treatment options, and particularly as documentation demands on clinicians continued to increase. I thought I did a good job of writing behavioral objectives, and then I met Art. Both Art and Jen stuck by me through my difficulties with "Plannerese" and my ADD style. Thank you!

It was particularly difficult with the sexual abuse topic to address treatment issues for victims and offenders in the same book. This was not my original plan, but the suggestion of Peggy Alexander at Wiley. With the change of plans, my focus became "No More Victims," and it became easy to conceptualize the structure of this Treatment Planner that included objectives for both victims and offenders. Peggy, thank you for your wisdom and grace.

I owe a debt of gratitude to a number of professional colleagues and friends for their support and critiques: my dear buddy, Jane Hollingsworth, Psy.D., who tirelessly gave research information, feedback, and friendship through this project and others; Sue Casselman, Psy.D., through short and long distances before and during this project was supportive, insightful, and my very good friend; Geoff Ludford, Ed.D., for his clinical wisdom and sense of humor; and Tom Plante, Ph.D., and Tim Horton, LCSW, both gave invaluable insight into their own treatment experiences with priests and other clerics. The Female Offenders chapter was enriched by the insights provided by Julia Hislop, Ph.D. (personal communication) and Barbara Schwartz, Ph.D. (conference presentation entitled "Looking Forward: Critical Issues in the Management of the Sex Offender," March 2002). David Cohen, M.A., at Magen Prison in Israel gave me his insights on Yetser HaRah. Two Virginia Beach probation officers par excellence, John Williams and Kate Shellman, also gave me useful feedback. And finally, credit is due to Bill Marshall for his pioneering work with sex offenders, along with other researchers and clinicians such as Tony Ward, Ph.D., Richard Laws, Ph.D., Steve Hudson, Ph.D., and Anna Salter, Ph.D.

In many ways, this was a family book, where all members contributed. Elizabeth and Christopher were understanding about changes in their routine and mostly understanding when they had to share the Internet with their mom. My husband, Bill, in his inimitable style reassured me many times, "Just go do it, I'll take care of dinner." And dear Mary, thanks for the weekends and doing the laundry. And thank you to Mom and Dad, who showed me right from the very beginning how to solve problems, how to heal, how to have joy, and how to love.

Finally, I'd like to thank all of the patients who have taught me, challenged me, and surprised me.

RITA BUDRIONIS

The Sexual Abuse Victim and Sexual Offender Treatment Planner, with DSM-5 Updates

INTRODUCTION

PLANNER FOCUS

The Sexual Abuse Victim and Sexual Offender Treatment Planner is designed to assist clinicians, social service workers, probation officers, and other professionals who are working with either survivors of sexual abuse/assault or the perpetrators of such crimes. The issues of these two groups are intertwined, as it is crucial for offenders to break through their denial and to acknowledge and empathize with the devastating harm that abuse has on the victims, and offenders are often victims of sexual abuse themselves. Important points of contact between these two groups are victim healing, victim safety, and a decreased recidivism rate.

This Planner can be used in a number of settings ranging from outpatient to residential to prison settings. Treatment objectives can be used for a wide range of clients ranging from juveniles to adults. Because offender treatment necessitates a melding of criminal justice concerns and psychological needs, many of the objectives and interventions will address collaboration with probation/parole officers.

Victim treatment is a specialized area of clinical expertise, although it is frequently encountered in the mental health field. This Planner can serve as the framework for the novice clinician to begin to build skills working with this population with the supervision of an experienced clinician. Victim treatment is frequently lengthy and demanding on both the client and therapist, and the difficulty increases with the severity of the trauma. This Planner assists in clarifying treatment options for the clinician in such critical areas as suicide and eating disorders, along with sensitive issues such as families with an impetus toward reunification and survivors with destabilizing trauma symptoms.

Treatment of sex offenders is a highly specialized area and based on a relatively recent body of research with many differing viewpoints and current controversies. When research data conflict or are not yet definitive, intervention choices are offered, such as in the Denial chapter where objective options range from programmatic discharge of a denying offender to placement into a pre-treatment denial group. In the Clergy Offender chapter, the bulk of the interventions are based on the clinical expertise of the generous professionals who shared their experiences with the authors. Overall, clinicians who treat sex offenders should receive extensive didactic training and clinical supervision. This Planner can serve as a support for the clinician who is licensed as a sex offender treatment provider or a clinician-in-training with such a population with the assistance of an experienced supervisor. Probation/parole officers, social service workers, and other professionals can use this Planner to evaluate current treatment needs, treatment progress, and the adequacy of programs that are available.

It is our goal to present information to assist in making clinical and programmatic decisions for psychotherapeutic treatment of those individuals who have been sexually assaulted and those individuals who are the perpetrators of sexual assault. Even the offender chapters, however, are victim-driven, maintaining the goal of victim support, healing, safety, and restorative justice. In this challenging and controversial area, our goal is a respectful treatment of all clients and "no more victims."

HISTORICAL BACKGROUND

Since the early 1960s, formalized treatment planning has gradually become a vital aspect of the entire health care delivery system, whether it is treatment related to physical health, mental health, child welfare, or substance abuse. What started in the medical sector in the 1960s spread into the mental health sector in the 1970s as clinics, psychiatric hospitals, agencies, and so on began to seek accreditation from bodies such as the Joint Commission on Accreditation of Healthcare Organizations (JCAHO) to qualify for third-party reimbursements. For most treatment providers to achieve accreditation, they had to begin developing and strengthening their documentation skills in the area of treatment planning. Previously, most mental health and substance abuse treatment providers had, at best, a bare-bones plan that looked similar for most of the individuals they treated. As a result, clients were uncertain as to what they were trying to attain in mental health treatment. Goals were vague, objectives were nonexistent, and interventions were applied equally to all clients. Outcome data were not measurable, and neither the treatment provider nor the client knew exactly when treatment was complete. The initial development of rudimentary treatment plans made inroads toward addressing some of these issues.

With the advent of managed care in the 1980s, treatment planning has taken on even more importance. Managed care systems *insist* that clinicians move rapidly from assessment of the problem to the formulation and implementation of the treatment plan. The goal of most managed care companies is to expedite the treatment process by prompting the client and treatment provider to focus on identifying and changing behavioral problems as quickly as possible. Treatment plans must be specific as to the problems and interventions, individualized to meet the client's needs and goals, and measurable in terms of setting milestones that can be used to chart the patient's progress. Pressure from third-party payers, accrediting agencies, and other outside parties has therefore increased the need for clinicians to produce effective, high-quality treatment plans in a short time frame. However, many mental health providers have little experience in treatment plan development. Our purpose in writing this book is to clarify, simplify, and accelerate the treatment planning process for youth involved in the juvenile justice system.

TREATMENT PLAN UTILITY

Detailed written treatment plans can benefit not only the client, therapist, treatment team, insurance community, and treatment agency, but also the overall psychotherapy profession. The client is served by a written plan because it stipulates the issues that are the focus of the treatment process. It is very easy for both provider and client to lose sight of what the issues were that brought the client into therapy. The treatment plan is a guide that structures the focus of the therapeutic contract. Because issues can change as therapy progresses, the treatment plan must be viewed as a dynamic document that can and must be updated to reflect any major change of problem, definition, goal, objective, or intervention.

Clients and therapists benefit from the treatment plan, which forces both to think about therapy outcomes. Behaviorally stated, measurable objectives clearly focus the treatment endeavor. Clients no longer have to wonder what therapy is trying to accomplish. Clear objectives also allow the client to channel effort into specific changes that will lead to the long-term goal of problem resolution. Therapy is no longer a vague contract to just talk honestly and openly about emotions and cognitions until the client feels better. Both client and therapist are concentrating on specifically stated objectives using specific interventions.

Providers are aided by treatment plans because they are forced to think analytically and critically about therapeutic interventions that are best suited for objective attainment for the client. Therapists were traditionally trained to "follow the patient," but now a formalized plan is the guide to the treatment process. The therapist must give advance attention to the technique, approach, assignment, or cathartic target that will form the basis for interventions.

Clinicians benefit from clear documentation of treatment because it provides a measure of added protection from possible patient litigation. Malpractice suits are increasing in frequency, and insurance premiums are soaring. The first line of defense against allegations is a complete clinical record detailing the treatment process. A written, individualized, formal treatment plan that is the guideline for the therapeutic process, that has been reviewed and signed by the client, and that is coupled with problem-oriented progress notes is a powerful defense against exaggerated or false claims.

A well-crafted treatment plan that clearly stipulates presenting problems and intervention strategies facilitates the treatment process carried out by team members in inpatient, residential, or intensive outpatient settings. Good communication between team members about what approach is being implemented and who is responsible for which intervention is critical. Team meetings to discuss patient treatment used to be the only source of interaction between providers; often, therapeutic conclusions or assignments were not recorded. Now, a thorough treatment plan stipulates in writing the details of objectives and the varied interventions (e.g., pharmacologic, milieu, group therapy, didactic, recreational, individual therapy) and who will implement them.

Every treatment agency or institution is constantly looking for ways to increase the quality and uniformity of the documentation in the clinical record. A standardized, written treatment plan with problem definitions, goals, objectives, and interventions in every client's file enhances that uniformity of documentation. This uniformity eases the task of record reviewers inside and outside the agency. Outside reviewers, such as JCAHO, insist on documentation that clearly outlines assessment, treatment, progress, and termination status.

The demand for accountability from third-party payers and health maintenance organizations (HMOs) is partially satisfied by a written treatment plan and complete progress notes. More and more managed care systems are demanding a structured therapeutic contract that has measurable objectives and explicit interventions. Clinicians cannot avoid this move toward being accountable to those outside the treatment process.

The psychotherapy profession stands to benefit from the use of more precise, measurable objectives to evaluate success in mental health treatment. With the advent of detailed treatment plans, outcome data can be more easily collected for interventions that are effective in achieving specific goals.

HOW TO DEVELOP A TREATMENT PLAN

The process of developing a treatment plan involves a logical series of steps that build on each other much like constructing a house. The foundation of any effective treatment plan is the data gathered in a thorough biopsychosocial assessment. As the client presents himself/herself for treatment, the clinician must sensitively listen to and understand what the client struggles with in terms of family-of-origin issues, current stressors, emotional status, social network, physical health, coping skills, interpersonal conflicts, self-esteem, and so on. Assessment data may be gathered from a social history, legal file physical exam, clinical interview, psychological testing, or contact with a client's guardian, social service worker, and/or probation officer. The integration of the data by the clinician or the multidisciplinary treatment team members is critical for understanding the client, as is an awareness of the basis of the client's struggle. We have identified six specific steps for developing an effective treatment plan based on the assessment data.

Step One: Problem Selection

Although the client may discuss a variety of issues during the assessment and court orders may request specific services, the clinician must ferret out the most significant problems on which to focus the treatment process. Usually a *primary* problem will surface, and *secondary* problems may also be evident. Some *other* problems may have to be set aside as not urgent enough to require treatment at this time. An effective treatment plan can only deal with a few selected problems, or treatment will lose its direction. *The Sexual Abuse Victim and Sexual Offender Treatment Planner* offers 27 problems from which to select those that most accurately represent your client's presenting issues.

As the problems to be selected become clear to the clinician or the treatment team, it is important to include opinions from the client as to his or her prioritization of issues for which help is being sought. A client's motivation to participate in and cooperate with the treatment process depends, to some extent, on the degree to which treatment addresses his or her greatest needs.

Step Two: Problem Definition

Each individual client presents with unique nuances as to how a problem behaviorally reveals itself in his or her life. Therefore, each problem that is selected for treatment focus requires a specific definition about how it is evidenced in the particular client. The symptom pattern should be associated with diagnostic criteria and codes such as those found in the *Diagnostic and Statistical Manual* (*DSM*-5) or the *International Classification of Diseases.* The Planner, following the pattern established by *DSM*-5, offers such behaviorally specific definition statements to choose from or to serve as a model for your own personally crafted statements. You will find several behavior symptoms or syndromes listed that may characterize 1 of the 32 presenting problems.

Step Three: Goal Development

The next step in treatment plan development is that of setting broad goals for the resolution of the target problem. These statements need not be crafted in measurable terms but can be global, long-term goals that indicate a desired positive outcome to the treatment procedures. The Planner suggests several possible goal statements for each problem, but one statement is all that is required in a treatment plan.

Step Four: Objective Construction

In contrast to long-term goals, objectives must be stated in behaviorally measurable language. It must be clear when the client has achieved the established objectives; therefore, vague, subjective objectives are not acceptable. Review agencies (e.g., JCAHO), HMOs, and managed care organizations insist that psychological treatment outcome be measurable. The objectives presented in this Planner are designed to meet this demand for accountability. Numerous alternatives are presented to allow construction of a variety of treatment plan possibilities for the same presenting problem. The clinician must exercise professional judgment as to which objectives are most appropriate for a given client.

Each objective should be developed as a step toward attaining the broad treatment goal. In essence, objectives can be thought of as a series of steps that, when completed, will result in the achievement of the long-term goal. There should be at least two objectives for each problem, but the clinician may construct as many as are necessary for goal achievement. Target attainment dates should be listed for each objective. New objectives should be added to the plan as the individual's treatment progresses. When all the necessary objectives have been achieved, the client should have resolved the target problem successfully.

Step Five: Intervention Creation

Interventions are the actions of the clinician designed to help the client complete the objectives. There should be at least one intervention for every objective. If the client does not accomplish the objective after the initial intervention, new interventions should be added to the plan.

Interventions should be selected on the basis of the client's needs and the treatment provider's full therapeutic repertoire. *The Sexual Abuse Victim and Sexual Offender Treatment Planner* contains interventions from a broad range of therapeutic approaches, including cognitive, dynamic, behavioral, multisystemic, pharmacologic, family-oriented, and client-centered therapy. Other interventions may be written by the provider to reflect his/her own training and experience. The addition of new problems, definitions, goals, objectives, and interventions to those found in the Planner is encouraged because doing so adds to the database for future reference and use.

Some suggested interventions listed in the Planner refer to specific books that can be assigned to the client for adjunctive bibliotherapy. Appendix A contains a full bibliographic reference list of these materials. The books are arranged under each problem for which they are appropriate as assigned reading for clients. When a book is used as part of an intervention plan, it should be reviewed with the client after it is read, enhancing the application of the content of the book to the specific client's circumstances. For further information about self-help books, mental health professionals may wish to consult *The Authoritative Guide to Self-Help Books* (1994) by Santrock, Minnett, and Campbell (available from The Guilford Press, New York).

A list of reference resources is also provided for the professional provider in Appendix B. These books are meant to elaborate on the methods suggested in some of the chapters.

Assigning an intervention to a specific provider is most relevant if the patient is being treated by a team in an inpatient, residential, or intensive outpatient setting. Within these settings, personnel other than the primary clinician may be responsible for implementing a specific intervention. Review agencies require that the responsible provider's name be stipulated for every intervention.

Step Six: Diagnosis Determination

The determination of an appropriate diagnosis is based on an evaluation of the client's complete clinical presentation. The clinician must compare the behavioral, cognitive, emotional, and interpersonal symptoms that the client presents to the criteria for diagnosis of a mental illness condition as described in *DSM-5*. The issue of differential diagnosis is admittedly a difficult one that research has shown to have rather low interrater reliability. Psychologists have also been trained to think more in terms of maladaptive behavior than disease labels. In spite of these factors, diagnosis is a reality that exists in the world of mental health care, and it is a necessity for third-party reimbursement. (However, recently, managed care agencies are more interested in behavioral indices that are exhibited by the client than the actual diagnosis.) It is the clinician's thorough knowledge of *DSM-5* criteria and a complete understanding of the client assessment data that contribute to the most reliable, valid diagnosis. An accurate assessment of behavioral indicators will also contribute to more effective treatment planning.

HOW TO USE THIS PLANNER

Our experience has taught us that learning the skills of effective treatment plan writing can be a tedious and difficult process for many clinicians. It is more stressful to try to develop this expertise when under the pressure of increased patient load and short time frames placed on clinicians today by managed care systems. The documentation demands can be overwhelming when we must move quickly from assessment to treatment plan to progress notes. In the process, we must be very specific about how and when objectives can be achieved, and how progress is exhibited in each client. *The Sexual Abuse Victim and Sexual Offender Treatment Planner* was developed as a tool to aid clinicians in writing a treatment plan in a rapid manner that is clear, specific, and highly individualized according to the following progression:

1. Choose one presenting problem (Step One) that you have identified through your assessment process. Locate the corresponding page number for that problem in the Planner's table of contents.
2. Select two or more of the listed behavioral definitions (Step Two), and record them in the appropriate section on your treatment plan form. Feel free to add your own defining statement if you determine that your client's behavioral manifestation of the identified problem is not listed. (Note that while our design for treatment planning is vertical, it will work equally well on plan forms formatted horizontally.)
3. Select a single long-term goal (Step Three), and again write the selection, exactly as it is written in the Planner or in some appropriately modified form, in the corresponding area of your own form.

4. Review the listed objectives for this problem, and select the ones that you judge to be clinically indicated for your client (Step Four). Remember, it is recommended that you select at least two objectives for each problem. Add a target date or the number of sessions allocated for the attainment of each objective.

5. Choose relevant interventions (Step Five). The Planner offers suggested interventions related to each objective in the parentheses following the objective statement. But do not limit yourself to those interventions. The entire list is eclectic and may offer options that are more tailored to your theoretical approach or preferred way of working with clients. Also, just as with definitions, goals, and objectives, there is space allowed for you to enter your own interventions into the Planner. This allows you to refer to these entries when you create a plan around this problem in the future. You will have to assign responsibility to a specific person for implementation of each intervention if the treatment is being carried out by a multidisciplinary team.

6. Several *DSM*-5 diagnoses are listed at the end of each chapter that are commonly associated with a client who has this problem. These diagnoses are meant to be suggestions for clinical consideration. Select a diagnosis listed, or assign a more appropriate choice from the *DSM*-5 (Step Six).

7. To accommodate those practitioners that tend to plan treatment in terms of diagnostic labels rather than presenting problems, Appendix B lists all of the *DSM*-5 diagnoses that have been presented in the various presenting problem chapters as suggestions for consideration. Each diagnosis is followed by the presenting problem that has been associated with that diagnosis. The provider may look up the presenting problems for a selected diagnosis to review definitions, goals, objectives, and interventions that may be appropriate for their clients with that diagnosis.

Congratulations! You should now have a complete, individualized treatment plan that is ready for immediate implementation and presentation to the client. It should resemble the format of the sample plan that follows.

A FINAL NOTE

One important aspect of effective treatment planning is that each plan should be tailored to the individual client's problems and needs. Treatment plans should not be mass-produced, even if clients have similar problems. The individual's strengths and weaknesses, unique stressors, social network, family circumstances, and symptom patterns *must* be considered in developing a treatment strategy. Drawing upon our own years of clinical experience, we have put together a variety of treatment choices. These statements can be combined in thousands of permutations to develop detailed treatment plans. Relying on their own good judgment, clinicians can easily select the statements that are appropriate for the individuals they are treating. In addition, we encourage readers to add their own definitions, goals, objectives, and interventions to the existing samples. It is our hope that *The Sexual Abuse Victim and Sexual Offender Treatment Planner* will promote effective, creative treatment planning—a process that will ultimately benefit the client, clinician, and mental health community.

SAMPLE TREATMENT PLAN

PROBLEM: SELF-BLAME

Definitions: Chronic and recurrent thoughts of blaming self for
the sexual abuse/trauma.
Feelings of inappropriate guilt and shame; views self
as damaged goods.

Goals: Decrease attribution of blame to self as having caused
or having any responsibility for the abuse/assault.
Place responsibility for the offense on the offender.

SHORT-TERM OBJECTIVES

1. Verbalize thoughts and feelings surrounding the sexual abuse.

2. Eliminate self-blame statements when talking about the abuse, and place blame on the offender.

THERAPEUTIC INTERVENTIONS

1. Explore the victim's incidents of sexual abuse victimization, allowing him/her to disclose only as much detail as he/she is comfortable with.

2. Monitor the victim's self-blame statements as he/she talks about the sexual abuse; gently highlight this self-blame when it occurs.

1. Have the victim practice verbalizations that assign blame to the offender for the sexual assault; use modeling to reframe self-blame statements.

2. Assist the victim in identifying his/her cognitive distortions that underlie the self-blame (e.g., "I was probably too friendly"; "I should have resisted more"; or "I am a bad person").

3. Verbalize an increased knowledge of how the perpetrator used manipulation before, during, and after the abuse to influence the attribution of the crime.

1. Teach the victim about manipulation and cognitive distortions used by sexual offenders in order to deny responsibility for the abuse (e.g., minimizing, blaming the victim, denial).

4. Express acceptance of the fact that by placing responsibility on the offender, feelings of anger and rage may increase.

1. Teach the victim that being angry with the perpetrator may be an essential part of the process of recovery and healing as blame is clearly placed on the offender.

5. Write a confrontation letter to the abuser to clarify that the abuser is responsible for the offense.

1. Assign the victim to write a letter (unsent) to the offender regarding feelings about abuse; critique the letter about appropriately assigning blame to the offender for abuse/assault.

6. Identify and replace dysfunctional thoughts about the abuse/assault that result in acceptance that the abuse was deserved or somehow a punishment for sin.

1. Ask the victim to keep a daily record of thoughts that are associated with shame and guilt, particularly noting those that are associated with deserving punishment and committing a sin.

2. Use logic and reality to challenge each dysfunctional assumption regarding having committed a sin or deserving punishment, replacing it with a realistic assumption.

Diagnosis: F43.21   Adjustment Disorder with Depressed Mood

Part 1

VICTIM ISSUES

ANGER DIFFICULTIES*

BEHAVIORAL DEFINITIONS

1. Unexpected and unpredictable feelings of rage have occurred since having been sexually abused.
2. History of suppression of anger regarding having been sexually abused, resulting in depression, self-destructive behaviors, or somatic symptoms.
3. Dissociation or numbing of feelings of anger toward the sexual offender.
4. History of explosive, aggressive outbursts that are out of proportion to precipitating stressors leading to assaultive acts or destruction of property.
5. Overreactions of hostility to insignificant irritants.
6. Use of verbally abusive language.
7. Body language or tense muscles (e.g., clenched fist or jaw, glaring looks, or refusal to make eye contact).
8. Use of passive-aggressive patterns (e.g., social withdrawal due to anger, lack of complete or timely compliance in following directions or rules, complaining about authority figures behind their backs, or nonparticipation in meeting expected behavioral norms).

—. _____

   _____

—. _____

   _____

—. _____

   _____

_____

*Much of the content of this chapter is adapted from "Anger Management" in *The Complete Adult Psychotherapy Treatment Planner* by A. Jongsma and L. M. Peterson, New York, John Wiley & Sons, 1999. Used with permission.

LONG-TERM GOALS

1. Accept the right to have and express anger toward the victim in ways that are self-empowering and healing.
2. Decrease overall intensity and frequency of angry feelings, and increase ability to recognize and appropriately express angry feelings as they occur.
3. Develop an awareness of current angry behaviors, clarifying origins of and alternatives to aggression, passive-aggressive behaviors, or suppression of anger.
4. Come to an awareness and acceptance of angry feelings while developing better control and more serenity.
5. Become capable of handling angry feelings in constructive ways that enhance daily functioning.

__. _____

_____

__. _____

_____

__. _____

_____

SHORT-TERM OBJECTIVES	THERAPEUTIC INTERVENTIONS
1. Verbally acknowledge experiencing feelings of anger. (1, 2)	1. Assist the victim in coming to the realization that he/she is angry by asking him/her to explore and label his/her feelings.
	2. Assign the victim to read the book *Of Course You're Angry* (Rosellini and Worden) or *The Angry Book* (Rubin).
2. Identify targets of and causes for anger in daily life. (2, 3, 4)	2. Assign the victim to read the book *Of Course You're Angry* (Rosellini and Worden) or *The Angry Book* (Rubin).

3. Verbalize an increased awareness of anger expression patterns. (5, 6)

4. Identify how significant others
in childhood have modeled
ways to handle anger. (7)

5. Identify the pain and hurt of
past or current life that fuels
ongoing anger. (8, 9)

6. Verbalize feelings of anger in a
controlled, assertive way. (10,
11, 12, 13)

3. Ask the victim to keep a daily
journal that documents actions, environmental events, or
internal thoughts that cause
anger, frustration, or irritation.

4. Assign the victim to write a
list of targets of and causes
for anger, and process this list
in session.

5. Gently confront the victim
about the transfer of angry
feelings toward the therapist,
either directly or indirectly,
such as indicated by missed
appointments, critical comments, or angry outbursts.

6. Refer the victim to an anger
management class or group.

7. Explore family-of-origin rules
regarding anger expression,
and use a genogram to identify
how significant others in childhood (e.g., parents, caretakers,
siblings, teachers) expressed
angry feelings.

8. Assign the victim to list the experiences of life that have hurt
and led to anger.

9. Empathize with and clarify the
victim's feelings of hurt and
anger tied to traumas of the
past.

10. Teach the victim assertiveness
skills, or assign him/
her assertiveness training
classes.

11. Process the victim's angry feelings or angry outbursts that have recently occurred, and review alternative behaviors that are available (e.g., taking a time-out, using deep breathing and relaxation techniques, speaking assertively but not aggressively, sharing feelings in writing or with a friend to diffuse anger).

12. Use role-playing techniques to assist the victim in developing non-self-defeating ways of handling angry feelings (e.g., assertive use of "I" messages).

13. Assign a specific exercise from an anger management workbook (e.g., *Dr. Weisinger's Anger Work Out Book* by Weisinger or *Skills Training Manual for Treating Borderline Personality Disorder* by Linehan), and process the exercise with the victim.

7. Use relaxation techniques to cope with angry feelings. (14)

14. Teach the victim relaxation techniques (e.g., deep breathing, positive guided imagery, deep muscle relaxation) to cope with initial response to angry feelings when they occur.

8. Verbalize an increased awareness of how maladaptive ways of expressing angry feelings have had a negative impact on self and others. (15, 16)

15. Ask the victim to list ways that the maladaptive expression of anger had resulted in negative consequences for himself/herself and others; process the list of consequences.

9. Identify the physical manifestations of anger, aggression, or violence. (11, 17, 18)

10. Report an increased awareness of anger triggers and the ability to react in a nonaggressive manner. (3, 19, 20)

16. Expand the victim's awareness of the negative effects that perpetually feeling angry has on his/her body and spirit.

11. Process the victim's angry feelings or angry outbursts that have recently occurred, and review alternative behaviors that are available (e.g., taking a time-out, using deep breathing and relaxation techniques, speaking assertively but not aggressively, sharing feelings in writing or with a friend to diffuse anger).

17. Encourage the victim to observe and label angry feelings while describing specific body sensations that are associated with the anger.

18. Review the victim's violent expressions of anger and the negative consequences for himself/herself and others (e.g., personal shame, distrust and fear from others, legal conflicts, injuries, loss of freedom, financial loss).

3. Ask the victim to keep a daily journal that documents actions, environmental events, or internal thoughts that cause anger, frustration, or irritation.

19. Assist the victim in developing the ability to recognize his/her triggers that lead to angry outbursts.

20. Help the victim to develop emotional regulation skills, which entails viewing anger as a wave that comes and goes and encourage a willingness to feel anger. (See *Skills Training Manual for Treating Borderline Personality Disorder* by Linehan.)

11. Write an angry letter to the target of anger, and process this letter with the therapist. (21, 22)

21. Ask the victim to write an angry letter to his/her sexual perpetrator, or whomever, focusing on the reasons for his/her anger toward that person. Process this letter in session.

22. Encourage the victim to express and release (while in session) feelings of anger, rage, and violent fantasies or plots for revenge.

12. Verbalize a recognition of how holding on to angry feelings, fighting them, or denying them increases emotional suffering. (16, 23)

16. Expand the victim's awareness of the negative effects that perpetually feeling angry has on his/her body and spirit.

23. Explore the victim's feelings about forgiving the offender, and help him/her see it as an option, not a requirement; explore the pros and cons. Address other options such as delaying the decision to forgive or not.

13. Write out the pros and cons of forgiving those who hurt self. (23, 24)

23. Explore the victim's feelings about forgiving the offender, and help him/her see it as an option, not a requirement; explore the pros and cons. Address other options such as delaying the decision to forgive or not.

24. Assign the victim to write a list of pressures to forgive the offender (e.g., urging by family members, financial and social pressures, guilt, or self-blame). (See the Self-Blame chapter in the Victim Issues part of this Planner.)

14. Clearly articulate anger toward the offender. (25, 26, 27)

25. Encourage the victim to explore whether he/she experiences self-blame for the abuse and to redirect appropriate anger at the offender. (See the Self-Blame chapter in the Victim Issues part of this Planner.)

26. Help the victim to see anger at the offender as part of the recovery process.

27. Listen empathically while the victim shares anger feelings about the offender while pointing out suppression or dissociation.

15. Verbalize the need and ability to control rage at the offender. (28, 29)

28. Assist the victim in understanding his/her feelings of rage toward the offender as an appropriate emotional response to the experience of being sexually assaulted, and separate this from violent actions.

29. Have the victim explore specific feelings of wanting to harm the offender and ask for an agreement not to physically harm anyone. Discuss the difference between feelings and behavior.

16. List some positive aspects of anger. (30, 31)

30. Explore with the victim how anger can be an appropriate response or signal to some environmental dangers (e.g., physical threat).

31. Ask the victim to list the positive aspects of anger (e.g., motivating him/her to take action or preventing another from doing something harmful).

17. Cooperate with a medication evaluation. (32)

32. Refer the victim for a medication evaluation if he/she appears overwhelmed, explosive, or out of control.

__. _____
   _____
__. _____

__. _____
   _____
__. _____

DIAGNOSTIC SUGGESTIONS:

ICD-9-CM	_ICD-10-CM_	_DSM-5_ Disorder, Condition, or Problem
312.34	F63.81	Intermittent Explosive Disorder
296.xx	F31.xx	Bipolar I Disorder
296.89	F31.81	Bipolar II Disorder
312.8	F91.x	Conduct Disorder
310.1	F07.0	Personality Change Due to Another Medical Condition
309.81	F43.10	Posttraumatic Stress Disorder
301.83	F60.3	Borderline Personality Disorder
301.7	F60.2	Antisocial Personality Disorder
301.0	F60.0	Paranoid Personality Disorder
301.81	F60.81	Narcissistic Personality Disorder
301.9	F60.9	Unspecified Personality Disorder
_____	_____	_____
_____	_____	_____

DISSOCIATION

BEHAVIORAL DEFINITIONS

1. An episode of inability to remember important information regarding the traumatic sexual abuse that is too extensive to be explained by ordinary forgetfulness.
2. Persistent or recurrent experiences of depersonalization, feeling automated or as if detached from or outside of one's mental processes or body, during which reality testing remains intact.
3. Persistent or recurrent experiences of derealization, feeling as if one is in a dream, where the environment feels unreal, strange, and unfamiliar.
4. Sudden, unexpected travel away from home with the inability to recall one's past, resulting in confusion about personal identity or assumption of a new identity.
5. The existence of two or more distinct personalities or personality states that recurrently take full control of one's behavior.

___. _____

_____

___. _____

_____

___. _____

_____

LONG-TERM GOALS

1. Resolve the emotional trauma that underlies the dissociative disturbance.
2. Reduce the frequency and duration of dissociative episodes.

3. Regain full memory.
4. Integrate the various personalities.
5. Reduce the level of daily distress caused by dissociative disturbances.

—. _____
_____

—. _____
_____

—. _____
_____

SHORT-TERM OBJECTIVES

THERAPEUTIC INTERVENTIONS

1. Describe the signs and symptoms that are experienced in the process of dissociation. (1, 2, 3)

1. Explore the victim's dissociative experiences, assessing the nature and extent of the symptoms (e.g., altered perception of time, space, and sense of self; confusion; flashbacks; numbing; amnesia; panic).

2. Administer a standardized or structured dissociative assessment technique to the victim (e.g., the Dissociative Experience Scale, the Dissociation Questionnaire, or the Dissociative Disorder Interview Schedule), and give him/her feedback.

3. Ask the victim to give a detailed description of the onset of the dissociative process.

2. Cooperate with a referral to a neurologist to rule out organic factors in amnestic episodes. (4)

4. Refer the victim to a neurologist for an evaluation of any organic cause for memory loss experiences.

3. Read material that is informative regarding dissociation to gain information about the condition. (5, 6)

4. Describe alternate personalities (alters) that function with some amount of autonomy. (7)

5. Implement the use of art and journal writing to gain a better understanding of the feelings and needs of each alter. (8, 9)

6. List ways that dissociation has been helpful in coping with the abuse. (10)

5. Ask the victim to read material on dissociation (e.g., *Courage to Heal* by Bass and Davis and/or *Multiple Personality Disorder from the Inside Out,* edited by Cohen, Giller, and Lynn); process these reading materials.

6. Educate the victim about the process of dissociation, that it is a coping strategy used by individuals who are predisposed to high hypnotizability in order to deal with painful affect and trauma.

7. Gently probe for information regarding alters and their role in the victim's emotional survival, being careful not to encourage increased dissociation.

8. Assign art and journal writing homework assignments to be completed by the victim's various alters as they appear; process these with him/her.

9. Teach the victim and his/her alters that integration is the general treatment goal, and help to decrease fears and resistance of the alters by assurances that integration will not lead to their annihilation.

10. Explore with the victim how dissociation helped him/her to survive when the sexual abuse was occurring and afterward.

7. Keep a journal of dissociative episodes. (11)

11. Assign the victim to keep a journal of daily thoughts, feelings, and dissociative experiences; pay special attention to precursors of the dissociative episodes.

8. Increase self-awareness feelings and thoughts by identifying emotionally stressful situations, which can elicit dissociation. (12)

12. Process with the victim his/her journal information to identify and work through emotionally stressful situations that have become precursors to dissociative episodes.

9. Work in a collaborative way with trusted family members and significant others to identify parameters of personality changes. (13)

13. Assign the victim to discuss dissociative experiences with one trusted social or family contact; process the sharing experience.

10. Cooperate with gradual exposure to stimuli that evoke dissociation. (14)

14. With the victim's input, develop and implement gradual exposure using a systemic desensitization hierarchy of nonabusive stimuli that are associated with the trauma and those that evoke dissociation.

11. Identify the somatic and emotional reactions that occur prior to and during dissociation. (15, 16)

15. Help the victim to identify the somatic reactions that occur prior to and during dissociation.

16. Help the victim to identify the strong emotions that trigger dissociation.

12. List alternate coping strategies to replace dissociation. (17)

17. Assist the victim in listing alternate responses to replace dissociation [e.g., writing out in a journal the descriptions of the thoughts of fear; implementing

13. Practice taking control of the dissociation process while in session. (18)

14. Implement techniques that demonstrate mastery over the dissociative experience. (19, 20, 21)

15. Reveal, explore, and talk about the history of the sexual abuse. (22)

tactile stimulation (e.g., holding ice or touching a rough texture); drawing a visual representation of thoughts and feelings of anxiety and fear], and practice these in the session.

18. As a way of practicing increasing control over dissociation, ask the victim to deliberately dissociate in the session and to note how the dissociation waxes and wanes.

19. Ask the victim to experiment at home with stimuli that will stop the dissociation (e.g., snapping a rubber band on the wrist, setting an alarm, splashing his/her face with cold water).

20. Give the victim homework sheets where he/she practices bringing himself/herself out of dissociation several times a day, rating how dissociated he/she was and how successful he/she was in stopping the dissociation.

21. Reinforce the victim for experiencing and acknowledging a sense of mastery and control over dissociative experiences.

22. Explore the victim's traumatic memories that are dissociated, assuming a supportive neutral stance regarding the accuracy of memories.

16. Verbalize a belief in own ability to endure painful affect without dissociating. (23, 24)

17. Practice intimacy skills by sharing personal art or written material regarding the sexual abuse with trusted significant others, group members, or family members. (25)

18. Use emotional regulation techniques as a way of gaining control over emotionality. (26)

19. Implement the use of a positive fantasy scene as a way to cope with a stressful situation. (27)

20. Use self-hypnosis as a collaborative tool to decrease anxiety, improve self-esteem, improve self-soothing skills, and encourage control of own fantasy life. (28, 29)

23. Acknowledge and reinforce the victim's ability to tolerate intense affect as he/she discusses the traumatic experiences in the session.

24. Encourage the victim in self-acceptance of his/her own feelings and thoughts and to take responsibility for his/her own behaviors.

25. Encourage the victim to share art or written material regarding his/her sexual abuse with trusted others as a way of building confidence, self-esteem, and improving stress tolerance.

26. Treat the victim for emotional lability. (See the Emotional Dysregulation chapter in the Victim Issues part of this Planner.)

27. Train the victim in positive guided imagery as a stress reduction technique (e.g., imagining himself/herself on a beach or in a forest).

28. Teach the victim about hypnosis/self-hypnosis, a facilitated, focused state of awareness, helping him/her become calmer and take more control of his/her fantasy life.

29. Use hypnosis/self-hypnosis to help the victim to reorient himself/herself to external reality, calm himself/

herself when his/her emotions are intense, and increase his/her self-esteem and confidence.

21. Using new coping strategies and without dissociation, discuss specific memories of abuse and the impact that the abuse had. (30)

22. Agree to cooperate with a reevaluation of the treatment plan during times of crisis, considering increased session frequency and hospitalization as viable options. (31)

23. Verbalize an acceptance that the treatment will be a long process when dealing with the goal of integrating alters. (32)

___. _____
_____
___. _____
_____
___. _____
_____

30. Help the victim to experience success in controlling dissociation in the session when discussing sexual trauma using new coping skills; reinforce calm mastery over emotions.

31. Increase sessions to two or three times per week if the victim becomes significantly destabilized during times of crisis. Assess for the need for hospitalization if he/she shows signs of being unable to attend to his/her basic needs.

32. Help the victim to accept that therapy with alters will be a long-term process in order to reach a point of stability and integration.

___. _____
_____
___. _____
_____
___. _____
_____

DIAGNOSTIC SUGGESTIONS:

ICD-9-CM	_ICD-10-CM_	_DSM-5_ Disorder, Condition, or Problem
303.90	F10.20	Alcohol Use Disorder, Moderate or Severe
300.14	F44.81	Dissociative Identity Disorder
300.6	F48.1	Depersonalization/Derealization Disorder
301.83	F60.3	Borderline Personality Disorder
301.9	F60.9	Unspecified Personality Disorder
_____	_____	_____
_____	_____	_____

EATING DISORDERS

BEHAVIORAL DEFINITIONS

1. Chronic, rapid consumption of large quantities of high-carbohydrate food.
2. Self-induced vomiting and/or abuse of laxatives due to fear of weight gain.
3. Extreme weight loss (and amenorrhea in females) with a refusal to maintain a minimal healthy weight.
4. Very limited ingestion of food and high frequency of secret, self-induced vomiting, inappropriate use of laxatives, and/or excessive strenuous exercise.
5. Persistent preoccupation with body image related to grossly inaccurate assessment of self as overweight, in spite of being normal or underweight.
6. Predominating irrational fear of becoming overweight.
7. Escalating fluid and electrolyte imbalance resulting from the eating disorder.
8. Strong denial of seeing self as emaciated even though severely under recommended weight.

__. _____
_____
__. _____
_____
__. _____
_____

LONG-TERM GOALS

1. Restore normal eating patterns, body weight, balanced fluid and electrolytes, and a realistic perception of body size and satiety.
2. Terminate the pattern of binge eating and purging behavior with a return to normal eating of enough nutritious foods to maintain a healthy weight.
3. Restructure the distorted thoughts, beliefs, and values that contribute to eating disorder development.
4. Gain an awareness of the interconnectedness of low self-esteem and society pressures with dieting, binge eating, and purging, in order to eliminate eating disorder behaviors.
5. Change the definition of self, so that it does not focus on weight, size, and shape as the primary criteria for self-acceptance.
6. Achieve a healthy goal weight at which point normal menstruation and ovulation occurs.

—. _____
_____

—. _____
_____

—. _____
_____

SHORT-TERM OBJECTIVES	THERAPEUTIC INTERVENTIONS
1. Describe the history and nature of eating patterns. (1, 2)	1. Gather a history of the victim's eating pattern (e.g., frequency, amounts, types of food).
	2. Evaluate and confront minimization or denial of eating-related problems.
2. Reveal dysfunctional behavior patterns engaged in that are related to food consumption. (2, 3)	2. Evaluate and confront minimization or denial of eating-related problems.

3. Explore the victim's use of dysfunctional behaviors to cope with concerns about eating and weight gain (e.g., vomiting, binging, purging, hoarding, laxative and diuretic use, excessive exercise).

3. Cooperate with a dental examination. (4)

4. Cooperate with a physical evaluation and verbalize acceptance of medical recommendations. (5, 6, 7)

4. Refer the victim for a dental examination in order to assess the need for remediation.

5. Refer the victim to a physician for a complete physical examination to rule out any undiagnosed medical condition and identify current medical needs (e.g., target weight range, vitamin deficiencies, somatic symptom evaluation).

6. Consult with the victim's physician to determine normal, healthy weight criteria (e.g., between 20 and 25 percent body fat, return of ovulation as determined by pelvic sonography, resumption of normal sexual and physical development).

7. Ask the victim to verbalize a commitment to follow the physician's recommendations.

5. Describe the nature of psychiatric symptoms experienced. (8)

8. Evaluate the victim for a comorbid psychiatric disorder (e.g., an affective disorder or anxiety), and address his/her treatment needs.

6. Cooperate with psychological testing. (9, 10)

7. Cooperate with a referral to evaluate the need for psychotropic medication, and comply with all recommendations. (11, 12)

8. Cooperate with admission to an inpatient treatment center if an evaluation indicates a need for such treatment. (13)

9. Identify fears of weight gain. (14, 15)

9. Administer psychological tests [e.g., the Minnesota Multiphasic Personality Inventory—2 (MMPI-2) or Beck Depression Inventory] to gain a clearer diagnostic picture of the victim's mental and emotional status.

10. Give the victim feedback on the psychological testing, and incorporate the results into the treatment plan.

11. Refer the victim to a physician for a medication evaluation to decrease depression and anxiety, to reduce the frequency of binge eating and purging, and to decrease the likelihood of relapse.

12. Encourage the victim to take the medication as prescribed and report on the side effects and effectiveness.

13. Arrange for hospitalization for the victim if there is a risk of suicide due to depression or a serious medical crisis due to low weight and a fragile physical condition.

14. Discuss the victim's fear of weight gain, and consult with his/her primary care physician regarding realistic weight goals.

15. Express empathic understanding for the victim regarding his/her feelings about the struggle with issues concerning weight; counter the victim's dysfunctional thoughts with realistic perceptions.

10. Cooperate with a dietician/
nutritionist to develop healthy
mean plans, minimum caloric
intake, and
implement these in daily life.
(16, 17)

11. Keep a journal of eating patterns, dysfunctional behaviors
related to eating, and the
thoughts and feelings associated with these behaviors. (18,
19)

12. Identify irrational feelings and
beliefs that impact eating patterns. (20, 21)

13. Set goals for daily food consumption, and keep a daily
journal of food consumed.
(22, 23)

16. Refer the victim to a
dietician/nutritionist for
assistance in initiating
adequate nutrition to
lead him/her to a realistic
weight, identify healthy eating
habits, and vanquish food-
related myths.

17. Process the results of the dieti-
cian's consultation, and identify the changes that the victim
should make, how he/she
could start implementing these
changes, and the feelings
around making these changes.

18. Assign the victim to keep a
daily journal of food consumption, laxative and
diuretic use, vomiting,
exercise, binging, and purging,
as well as the thoughts and
feelings that are associated
with these behaviors.

19. Teach the victim to accurately
perceive hunger and satiety
through the use of rating
hunger levels in his/her daily
eating journal.

20. Assist the victim in identifying
and exploring his/her emotions that lead to dysfunctional eating behavior.

21. Process the victim's negative
cognitive messages (e.g., catastrophizing or exaggerating)
that mediate his/her avoidance
of food intake.

22. Assist the victim in setting
daily food consumption goals,
and assign him/her to keep
daily journal entries of food
consumed; process in session
and adjust daily criteria, as
necessary.

14. Verbalize positive self-talk in session, and practice frequently during the daily routine. (24, 25, 26, 27, 28)

23. Teach the victim coping strategies (e.g., positive affirmations, daily meditation, support group attendance) to use in ameliorating the anxiety of eating normally and maintaining a normal weight without using eating disorder behaviors.

24. Reinforce the victim's positive verbalizations about himself/herself in session through the use of praise and verbal support.

25. Assign the victim to complete self-esteem-building exercises [e.g., listing positive traits and accomplishments (such as those found in *Building Blocks of Self-Esteem* by Shapiro) or a selected individual exercise].

26. Ask the victim to complete and process an exercise in the book *Ten Days to Self-Esteem!* (Burns).

27. Assist the victim in developing positive self-talk as a way of boosting his/her confidence and self-image.

28. Assign mirror exercises where the victim talks positively about himself/herself.

15. Identify distorted body perceptions and replace them with more realistic, healthy perceptions. (21, 29)

21. Process the victim's negative cognitive messages (e.g., catastrophizing or exaggerating) that mediate his/her avoidance of food intake.

29. Challenge the victim's distorted body image by discussion and assignment of relevant reading materials (e.g., *Body Traps* by Rodin or *Feeding the Hungry Heart— The Experience of Compulsive Eating* by Roth).

16. Implement new communication and assertiveness skills. (30, 31)

30. Enhance the victim's relationship skills by training him/her in assertiveness and problem-solving skills.

31. Teach the victim communication skills (e.g., how to make "I" statements, fair-fighting techniques, and feelings expression).

17. Verbalize an understanding of how eating disorder behaviors can bring a false sense of self-control and temporary alleviation of negative emotions. (32)

32. Teach the victim that, as a victim of sexual abuse, eating disorder behaviors can bring a false sense of self-control and temporary alleviation of negative emotions (e.g., guilt, anger, and self-disgust).

18. Acknowledge and overcome the role that dysfunctional family patterns have in the initiation and maintenance of eating disorder behaviors. (33, 34, 35)

33. Help the victim to identify family patterns of interaction that contribute to the maintenance of the eating disorder.

34. Assist the victim in completing a family genogram that focuses on a family history of eating patterns and messages about food and body weight.

35. In a family therapy session, focus on issues related to emotional support for each other and remediation of communication difficulties.

19. Verbalize an insight regarding separation and emancipation issues related to the family of origin. (36)

20. Attend eating disorder group therapy meetings in order to support recovery. (37)

21. Identify sources of ongoing support to help in maintaining gains and constructively dealing with triggers for food obsessions, dysfunctional behaviors, and emotional distress. (38, 39)

22. Verbalize an acceptance of body flaws and imperfections. (40, 41)

36. Address the victim's separation issues, discussing his/her feelings toward becoming independent from the family, and family cognitive messages regarding dependency and emancipation.

37. Recommend that the victim attend group counseling that is specifically designed to address eating disorder issues.

38. Refer the victim to Internet message boards and online chat groups that are pro-recovery, and teach him/her to avoid those that support dysfunctional thinking or dispense misinformation; process the information that is collected, dispelling myths and correcting cognitive distortions.

39. Refer the victim to an eating disorders support group (e.g., Eating Disorders Anonymous with information on the Internet at www .eatingdisordersanonymous .org) in order to help him/her get emotional support, decrease shame surrounding the disease, and increase his/her self-esteem.

40. Confront the victim's perfectionistic standards regarding body image, and establish realistic cognitions to develop a positive body image.

41. Assign behavioral exercises that are targeted to improve body image (e.g., positive self-talk, asking for positive feedback from support persons, shopping for flattering clothes and accessories).

23. Implement coping strategies to reduce emotionality. (42)

24. Identify potential relapse triggers, and list strategies for constructively coping with each trigger. (43)

42. Address emotional dysregulation, which can be a major trigger of binge eating and purging; assist the victim in listing constructive ways to reduce emotionality. (See the Emotional Dysregulation chapter in the Victim Issues part of this Planner.)

43. Assist the victim in identifying factors that lead to a relapse of eating disorder behaviors; outline relapse prevention strategies (e.g., stress management techniques, continuing contact with support persons, individual and family therapy).

__. _____
    _____
__. _____
    _____
__. _____
    _____

__. _____
    _____
__. _____
    _____
__. _____
    _____

DIAGNOSTIC SUGGESTIONS:

ICD-9-CM	_ICD-10-CM_	_DSM-5_ Disorder, Condition, or Problem
307.1	F50.02	Anorexia Nervosa, Binge-Eating/Purging Type
307.1	F50.01	Anorexia Nervosa, Restricting Type
307.51	F50.2	Bulimia Nervosa
307.50	F50.9	Unspecified Feeding or Eating Disorder
301.6	F60.7	Dependent Personality Disorder
_____	_____	_____
_____	_____	_____

EMOTIONAL DYSREGULATION

BEHAVIORAL DEFINITIONS

1. Under minor stress occurs extreme emotional reactivity that usually does not last more than a few hours to a few days.
2. Frequent eruptions of intense, inappropriate anger.
3. Chronic feelings of emptiness and boredom.
4. A history of intense, chaotic interpersonal relationships.
5. Chronic feelings of emotional vulnerability.
6. Engages in impulsive behaviors that are potentially self-damaging as a way to deal with painful emotions (e.g., binge eating, substance use, hypersexuality).
7. Recurrent suicidal gestures, threats, or self-mutilating behavior.
8. Easily believes that others are treating him/her unfairly or that they can't be trusted.
9. Difficulty in coping with stress and frequently blames others for making unreasonable demands.
10. Sets unrealistic expectations and unreasonable goals for self, feeling shame and guilt when failing to meet these.
11. Becomes very anxious with any hint of perceived abandonment in a relationship.

__. _____
   _____

__. _____
   _____

__. _____
   _____

LONG-TERM GOALS

1. Develop and implement coping skills to deal with mood swings.
2. Develop the ability to control impulses.
3. Learn and demonstrate strategies to deal with dysphoric moods.
4. Develop and implement emotional regulation and anger management skills.
5. Learn and practice interpersonal relationship skills and improve social adjustment.
6. Terminate self-damaging behaviors (e.g., substance abuse, reckless driving, sexual acting out, binge eating, parasuicidal, or suicidal behaviors).

__. _____
   _____
__. _____
   _____
__. _____
   _____

SHORT-TERM OBJECTIVES

1. Describe the nature, history, and causes for emotional dysregulation. (1, 2)

THERAPEUTIC INTERVENTIONS

1. Gather a history of the victim's emotional lability, interpersonal conflicts, self-damaging behaviors, and anger symptoms.

2. Teach the victim the origins of emotional dysregulation (biological and environmental factors and their interactions during childhood) and the resulting difficulties (e.g., mood instability, tendency toward substance abuse, and difficulty to tolerate any strong emotion).

2. Report feeling accepted by the therapist, and verbalize a commitment to participate in treatment. (3, 4, 5)

3. Express empathic acceptance of the victim while confronting dysfunctional behaviors (e.g., suicidal gestures, self-mutilation, substance abuse).

4. Support the victim by accurate reflection of feelings to validate his/her feelings and increase his/her trust in the therapeutic relationship.

5. Develop the goals of therapy in a collaborative manner, orienting the victim to the concept of a treatment contract and addressing his/her needs and dissatisfactions and the therapist's limitations regarding tolerating missed appointments, suicidal gestures, and demanding behavior; set clear guidelines.

3. Verbalize an understanding of the cyclic nature of impulsive behavior leading to guilt and shame, which lead to more impulsive behavior. (6, 7)

6. Facilitate the victim's understanding that impulsive behaviors can bring temporary relief from negative affect, but usually make him/her feel worse not long after the short respite from intense affect.

7. Address how impulsive behaviors ultimately lead to shame and guilt later and a cyclic increase in more impulsive behavior to alleviate the guilt.

4. Reframe dysfunctional behavior and verbalize an acceptance of self. (8)

8. Point out that the victim's dysfunctional actions (e.g., attempting to manipulate, seeking attention, sabotaging treatment) are an effort to reduce negative affect and to feel better.

5. Verbalize a commitment to terminate self-destructive behaviors. (9)

6. Cooperate with a referral to a physician to evaluate the need for psychotropic medication. (10)

7. Take medication as prescribed on a regular, consistent basis, reporting as to the side effects and effectiveness. (11)

8. Describe honestly the extent of engaging in dysfunctional or self-destructive behaviors. (12)

9. Consent to giving information to and cooperating with consultation from other professionals as part of the treatment process. (13)

10. Identify cognitive methods of increasing tolerance for intense affect. (14)

9. Solicit the victim's agreement that he/she will work to decrease suicidal and parasuicidal behaviors and other behaviors that interfere with treatment (e.g., substance abuse, prostitution, manipulation).

10. Refer the victim to a psychiatrist to evaluate his/her mood instability and to consider prescribing psychotropic medications.

11. Monitor the victim's compliance with the physician's prescription for psychotropic medication; consult with the physician as to the effectiveness and side effects.

12. Thoroughly assess the victim for other significant psychopathology (e.g., compulsive gambling, prostitution, shoplifting).

13. Use a team approach in treating the victim, consulting colleagues, including the victim's psychiatrist, primary care physician, group therapy leader, and support network.

14. Assign the victim to complete homework exercises on understanding and coping with strong feelings (e.g., Chapter 1 in *Surviving Childhood Sexual Abuse Workbook* by Ainscough and Toon); process the methods learned.

11. Read material that is informative regarding borderline personality disorder to gain knowledge about the condition. (15)

12. Cooperate with an assessment of and treatment plan for suicidal ideation and impulses. (16)

13. Verbalize a commitment to report urges to self-injure, and use coping strategies to avoid acting on impulses. (17)

14. Journal the daily level of self-abuse urges, negative and positive behaviors engaged in, and intensity of positive and negative emotions. (18, 19)

15. Refer the victim to books (e.g., *Lost in the Mirror: An Inside Look at Borderline Personality Disorder* by Moskovitz and *The Angry Heart: Overcoming Borderline and Addictive Disorders: An Interactive Self-Help Guide* by Santoro and Cohen) and Internet sources (e.g., www.psychcentral.com) that can provide information about borderline personality disorder.

16. Address the victim's suicidal ideation and gestures by asking him/her to agree to a contract for his/her safety. (See the Suicidal Ideation/Attempt chapter in the Offender and Victim Issues part of this Planner.)

17. Teach the victim problem-solving strategies regarding coping with self-injury behavior and ideation. (See the Self-Injury chapter in the Victim Issues part of this Planner.)

18. Teach the victim how to label and regulate emotional states by giving homework exercises of journaling feelings, thoughts, and behavior. (See the "Emotional Regulation" handouts in *Skills Training Manual for Treating Borderline Personality Disorder* by Linehan.)

19. Teach the victim that he/she must learn to tolerate some emotional pain and recognize that it will ebb and flow.

15. Develop and implement a personal metaphor as a technique for coping with intense affect. (20)

16. Report increased confidence in own ability to manage affect through the use of cognitive-behavioral and distress tolerance strategies. (21, 22)

17. Implement effective social skills to improve relationships. (23, 24)

20. Help the victim to create a metaphor that has personal impact on how to deal effectively with intense emotions (e.g., emotions are like clouds passing by in the sky or a wave rolling by on the ocean; observe them; do not try to make them bigger or smaller or judge them, but accept them); encourage him/her to use this metaphor for coping with urges and feelings.

21. Teach the victim to use distress tolerance skills as an alternative way to find relief from intense affect. (See *Skills Training Manual for Treating Borderline Personality Disorder* by Linehan.)

22. Assist the victim in developing a cue card to prompt himself/herself to focus on sensory experiences (e.g., What sounds do you hear? What colors do you see? What are the textures that you can feel that are within your reach?) as a way of living in the here and now. (See *Skills Training Manual for Treating Borderline Personality Disorder* by Linehan.)

23. Teach the victim how to be respectful of others in interpersonal interactions.

24. Teach the victim social skills (e.g., using "I" messages, assertiveness, and eye contact). (See the Social Withdrawal chapter in the Victim Issues part of this Planner.)

18. Learn ways to self-soothe, concentrate on the here and now, and reduce distracting thoughts and evaluations. (22, 25, 26)

22. Assist the victim in developing a cue card to prompt himself/herself to focus on sensory experiences (e.g., What sounds do you hear? What colors do you see? What are the textures that you can feel that are within your reach?) as a way of living in the here and now. (See *Skills Training Manual for Treating Borderline Personality Disorder* by Linehan.)

25. Instruct the victim in mindfulness skills to assist him/her in balancing and regulating emotions. (See *Skills Training Manual for Treating Borderline Personality Disorder* by Linehan.)

26. Help the victim accept himself/herself and reality without judgment by using positive cognitive affirmations and meditation.

19. Attend and participate in group therapy focusing on borderline personality issues. (27, 28)

27. Refer the victim to a weekly dialectical behavioral skills training group. (See *Skills Training Manual for Treating Borderline Personality Disorder* by Linehan.)

28. Review the lessons learned by the victim in the dialectical behavioral skills group; reinforce their use in his/her daily life.

20. Identify triggers of dysfunctional behaviors, and develop strategies for constructively dealing with each trigger. (29)

29. Periodically reevaluate with the victim the triggers for the behaviors that continue to interfere with therapy; develop strategies to cope with these triggers.

21. Use telephone consultation to get encouragement from the therapist, limiting the time and topic discussion as directed by the treatment plan. (30)

22. Verbalize an acceptance of limits set by others without falling back on dysfunctional coping mechanisms. (31, 32)

23. Disclose incidents of abuse or neglect and the symptoms that have resulted from these traumas. (33)

24. Participate in community or religious organizations that offer opportunities for service to others. (34)

30. Set up a telephone consultation schedule in order to provide support to the victim to increase the likelihood of the generalization skills to daily living. Set a clear time and topic limits.

31. Inform the victim that a completely unconditional, therapeutic relationship is not possible and that limits must be set, that he/she has the ability to violate boundaries and exhibit behaviors that will result in the therapist rejecting him/her; point out situations where boundaries have been crossed, and work on specific skills that will result in more effective and appropriate behaviors.

32. Assign the victim to read material on setting and accepting personal boundaries. (See *Where to Draw the Line: How to Set Healthy Boundaries Every Day* by Katherine.)

33. Explore with the victim his/her history of sexual, physical, and emotional abuse, and address posttraumatic stress disorder (PTSD) symptoms. [See the Posttraumatic Stress Disorder (PTSD) chapter in the Victim Issues part of this Planner.]

34. Refer the victim to supportive organizations (e.g., religious, charitable, or social service organizations) that will continue to encourage him/her to live a happy existence/life through giving of himself/herself to help others, rather than focus totally on himself/herself.

—. _____   —. _____
   _____   _____
—. _____   —. _____
   _____   _____
—. _____   _____

DIAGNOSTIC SUGGESTIONS:

ICD-9-CM	_ICD-10-CM_	_DSM-5_ Disorder, Condition, or Problem
309.81	F43.10	Posttraumatic Stress Disorder
296.xx	F32.x	Major Depressive Disorder, Single Episode
296.xx	F33.x	Major Depressive Disorder, Recurrent Episode
300.4	F34.1	Persistent Depressive Disorder
300.14	F44.81	Dissociative Identity Disorder
303.90	F10.20	Alcohol Use Disorder, Moderate or Severe
305.00	F10.10	Alcohol Use Disorder, Mild
304.30	F12.20	Cannabis Use Disorder, Moderate or Severe
305.20	F12.10	Cannabis Use Disorder, Mild
304.20	F14.20	Cocaine Use Disorder, Moderate or Severe
305.60	F14.10	Cocaine Use Disorder, Mild
305.70	F15.10	Amphetamine Use Disorder, Mild
304.40	F15.20	Amphetamine Use Disorder, Moderate or Severe
305.50	F11.10	Opioid Use Disorder, Mild
304.00	F11.20	Opioid Use Disorder, Moderate or Severe
305.90	F18.10	Inhalant Use Disorder, Mild
304.60	F18.20	Inhalant Use Disorder, Moderate or Severe
296.89	F31.81	Bipolar II Disorder
301.83	F60.3	Borderline Personality Disorder
301.9	F60.9	Unspecified Personality Disorder

_____ _____ _____

_____ _____ _____

POSTTRAUMATIC STRESS DISORDER (PTSD)

BEHAVIORAL DEFINITIONS

1. Exposure to acts of sexual abuse/assault (along with physical or psychological abuse) directed toward the victim that resulted in an intense emotional response of fear, helplessness, or horror.
2. Intrusive, distressing thoughts or images or sensory flashbacks that relive the traumatic event.
3. Disturbing dreams associated with the sexual trauma.
4. A sense that the events are reoccurring, as in illusions or flashbacks.
5. Intense distress when exposed to reminders of the sexual abuse.
6. Physiological reactivity when exposed to internal or external cues that symbolize the abuse.
7. Avoidance of thoughts, feelings, or conversations about the sexual trauma.
8. Avoidance of activity, places, or people associated with the sexual trauma.
9. Inability to recall some important aspect of the sexual abuse.
10. Lack of interest and participation in significant life activities.
11. A sense of detachment from others.
12. Inability to experience the full range of emotions, including love.
13. A pessimistic, fatalistic attitude regarding the future.
14. Sleep disturbance.
15. Irritability.
16. Autonomic hyperarousal.
17. Lack of concentration.
18. Hypervigilance.
19. Exaggerated startle response.

20. Sad or guilty affect and other signs of depression.
21. Alcohol and/or drug abuse.
22. Suicidal thoughts.
23. A pattern of interpersonal conflict, especially in intimate relationships.
24. Verbally and/or physically violent threats or behavior.
25. Inability to maintain employment due to authority/coworker conflict or anxiety symptoms.
26. Symptoms have been present for more than one month.

__. _____
   _____
   _____

__. _____
   _____
   _____

__. _____
   _____
   _____

LONG-TERM GOALS

1. Reduce the negative impact that the trauma of sexual abuse/assault has had on many aspects of life and improve functioning.
2. Develop and implement effective coping skills to carry out normal responsibilities and participate constructively in relationships.
3. Recall the sexual trauma events without becoming overwhelmed with negative emotions.
4. Terminate the destructive behaviors that serve to maintain escape and denial while implementing behaviors that promote healing, acceptance of the past events, and responsible living.

__. _____
   _____
   _____

__. _____
   _____
   _____

__. _____
   _____

SHORT-TERM OBJECTIVES	THERAPEUTIC INTERVENTIONS
1. Cooperate with and complete psychological testing to help evaluate trauma symptoms. (1)	1. Administer or refer for administration of psychological testing to assess for the presence and strength of PTSD symptoms [e.g., Minnesota Multiphasic Personality Inventory—2 (MMPI-2); Impact of Events Scale; Clinician Administered PTSD Scales—I (CAPS-I); Trauma Symptom Checklist; Posttraumatic Cognitions Inventory (PTCI)].
2. Describe the signs and symptoms of PTSD that are experienced and how they interfere with daily living. (2, 3)	2. Ask the victim to identify how the sexual trauma has negatively impacted his/her life.
	3. Ask the victim to list and then rank the order of the strength of his/her symptoms of PTSD.
3. Identify negative coping strategies that have been used to cope with the feelings associated with the trauma. (4)	4. Evaluate with the victim what negative coping strategies he/she has used in dealing with PTSD symptoms (e.g., substance abuse, anger outbursts, social isolation, avoidance of any reminder or thoughts of the abuse).
4. Identify internal and external stimuli that trigger PTSD symptoms. (5, 6, 7)	5. Ask the victim to identify what parts of his/her conscious memories are the most distressing and act as triggers for stress symptoms.
	6. Assign the victim to list what environmental stimuli evoke the most the most distressing symptoms; suggest that he/she keep a journal of instances of stress being triggered.

7. Assign the victim to identify triggers to feelings that are associated with the sexual trauma by completing exercises in the *Surviving Childhood Sexual Abuse Workbook* (Ainscough and Toon); process the material that is produced.

5. Verbalize an acceptance that trauma symptoms are common and can originate in abusive childhood experiences. (8, 9)

8. Explain to the victim that PTSD symptoms (e.g., autonomic hyperarousal and intrusive memories) are part of the normal coping process that occurs with any traumatic abnormal event.

9. Explain to the victim that exposure to prolonged early trauma (e.g., childhood sexual abuse) may result in brain and hormonal changes that can lead to difficulties with memory, learning, emotional regulation, poor impulse control or depression that carry on into adulthood.

6. Verbalize an understanding of the fact that recurring memories of trauma rarely cease completely and that coping with them is a lifelong process. (10, 11)

10. Help the victim to accept that healing from trauma is not the same as forgetting and that memories of the abuse will wax and wane over his/her life.

11. Encourage the victim to accept that sexual trauma memories will not be erased as the result of therapy; however, life can become manageable.

7. Acknowledge that healing from PTSD is a gradual process. (12, 13)

12. Outline the treatment process to the victim, explaining that it will include a gradual processing of the details and feelings associated with the trauma and developing new, more appropriate coping strategies.

8. Verbalize the strong emotions that are associated with the sexual trauma. (14)

9. Describe any signs and symptoms of dissociation that are experienced. (15)

10. Cooperate with the eye movement desensitization and reprocessing (EMDR) technique to reduce emotional reaction to the traumatic event. (16)

11. Identify coping strategies to deal with trauma memories and the associated emotional reaction. (17)

12. Cooperate with a medication evaluation by accurately reporting suicidal ideation, depression, anxiety, or disruptive emotional symptoms, if present. (18)

13. Follow a medication regimen as recommended by the physician, and report any side effects that are experienced. (19)

13. Educate the victim as to the origins of PTSD, common symptoms, and how it affects abuse survivors.

14. Explore the victim's strong feelings (e.g., shame, guilt, and anger), which are common feelings for abuse and other trauma survivors.

15. Assess whether the victim experiences dissociative symptoms (e.g., flashbacks, memory loss, identity disorder), and treat or refer for treatment. (See the Dissociation chapter in the Victim Issues part of this Planner.)

16. Use the EMDR technique to reduce emotional reactivity.

17. Teach the victim coping strategies (e.g., writing down thoughts and feelings in a journal; taking deep, slow breaths; calling a support person to talk about memories) to deal with trauma memories and sudden emotional reactions without becoming emotionally numb or feeling overwhelmed and out of control.

18. Refer the victim to a psychiatrist for a consultation regarding medication management of symptoms.

19. Process with the victim the results of the psychiatric evaluation and medication recommendations; encourage

14. Participate in developing a concrete plan for increasing social contacts in order to form a social support network. (20, 21, 22)

15. Reduce the amount and frequency of using mood-altering substances. (23)

16. Comply with an evaluation and treatment for chemical dependency. (24)

17. Participate in a desensitization procedure in which gradual exposure to nonharmful stimuli that are associated with the abuse is initiated. (25, 26)

him/her to comply with these recommendations and report any side effects as they occur.

20. Encourage the victim to slowly increase interpersonal contacts with supportive family members and significant others who were not responsible for the sexual trauma.

21. Encourage the victim to slowly increase overall social contacts, decreasing isolation from others in general; devise a plan and list of such contacts.

22. Assist the victim in identifying a support system of people with whom he/she can talk when feeling overwhelmed.

23. Teach the victim how to manage urges to use alcohol or drugs when feeling overwhelmed by flashbacks (e.g., attend a 12-step meeting, call a sponsor, engage in exercise).

24. Assess the depth of the victim's substance abuse pattern; refer or treat the victim for chemical dependence. (See the Substance Abuse chapter in the Offender and Victim Issues part of this Planner.)

25. Use a systemic desensitization procedure to gradually expose the victim to nonharmful stimuli that are associated with the sexual abuse.

26. Help the victim to challenge thoughts that something horrible will happen if he/she experiences a flashback while participating in the desensitization procedure; focus him/her on more positive coping thoughts.

18. Practice relaxation methods that do not increase the physical sensations associated with the abuse. (27)

27. Teach the victim a relaxation or calming technique (e.g., meditation, yoga, deep breathing techniques, prayer, and progressive relaxation) that he/she can institute as a daily ritual.

19. Make a list of 20 distracting techniques, and practice using them when feelings become overwhelming. (28)

28. Assist the victim in listing 20 ways that he/she could distract himself/herself (e.g., take a warm bath, listen to soothing music, sing a song or church hymn) when flashbacks or feelings become intense.

20. Verbalize an increased sense of mastery over PTSD symptoms by using a number of techniques to cope with flashbacks, decrease the power of triggers, and decrease negative thinking. (29, 30, 31, 32)

29. Increase the victim's confidence in coping with PTSD symptoms by assigning him/her to list at least two positive actions or small successes daily in a journal; process these success experiences.

30. Assist the victim in retelling abuse experiences to a therapist and to significant others in sessions as a means of gaining a feeling of mastery over PTSD.

31. Assign the victim to read about other trauma survivors (e.g., holocaust victims or war veterans) and some of the coping strategies they use. (See *The Color Purple* by Walker and *When Bad Things Happen to Good People* by Kushner.)

32. Assign the victim to write a list of positive affirmations (e.g., "I love and accept myself more and more each day"; "I will overcome this trauma and become a strong survivor"; recite a short, positive verse from the Bible or other spiritual writing), put the list up at home, and read them at least once per day.

21. Articulate in writing a stress inoculation plan for coping with environmental stressors. (33)

33. Assist the victim in developing a stress-hardy lifestyle to include critical elements (e.g., seeing stressors, such as holidays, school exams, or visits from relatives, as challenges and opportunities; daily reviewing his/her commitment to family, home, and personal growth; exercising regularly) and eating nutritious meals.

22. Implement the use of physical exercise on a daily basis in order to reduce PTSD symptoms and increase the sense of control and mastery over the body. (34)

34. Help the victim to start participating in a physical program (e.g., exercise or dance) where he/she can feel more competent and more in control of his/her body.

23. Increase involvement in positive, pleasurable activities. (35)

35. Explore with the victim his/her interests in cultural, artistic, or athletic activities; list those activities in which he/she can commit to increasing his/her involvement.

24. Increase involvement in community service activities on a volunteer basis. (36)

36. Encourage the victim to become involved in creative outlets by giving something back to the community, as opposed to a life script of avoiding triggering stimuli.

25. Join a support group with other abuse survivors, and commit to a six-month attendance. (37)

37. Encourage the victim to join a sexual abuse or sexual trauma support group.

___. _____   ___. _____
      _____   _____
___. _____   ___. _____
      _____   _____
___. _____   ___. _____
      _____   _____

DIAGNOSTIC SUGGESTIONS:

ICD-9-CM	_ICD-10-CM_	_DSM-5_ Disorder, Condition, or Problem
309.81	F43.10	Posttraumatic Stress Disorder
300.14	F44.81	Dissociative Identity Disorder
300.15	F44.9	Unspecified Dissociative Disorder
300.15	F44.89	Other Specified Dissociative Disorder
309.0	F43.21	Adjustment Disorder, With Depressed Mood
995.53	T74.22XA	Child Sexual Abuse, Confirmed, Initial Encounter
995.53	T74.22XD	Child Sexual Abuse, Confirmed, Subsequent Encounter
995.83	T74.21XA	Spouse or Partner Violence, Sexual, Confirmed, Initial Encounter
995.83	T74.21XD	Spouse or Partner Violence, Sexual, Confirmed, Subsequent Encounter
995.83	T74.21XA	Adult Sexual Abuse by Nonspouse or Nonpartner, Confirmed, Initial Encounter
995.83	T74.21XD	Adult Sexual Abuse by Nonspouse or Nonpartner, Confirmed, Subsequent Encounter
995.54	T74.12XA	Child Physical Abuse, Confirmed, Initial Encounter
995.54	T74.12XD	Child Physical Abuse, Confirmed, Subsequent Encounter
V61.12	Z69.12	Encounter for Mental Health Services for Perpetrator of Spouse or Partner Violence, Physical

V62.83	Z69.82	Encounter for Mental Health Services for Perpetrator of Nonspousal Adult Abuse
308.3	F43.0	Acute Stress Disorder
303.90	F10.20	Alcohol Use Disorder, Moderate or Severe
305.00	F10.10	Alcohol Use Disorder, Mild
304.30	F12.20	Cannabis Use Disorder, Moderate or Severe
305.20	F12.10	Cannabis Use Disorder, Mild
304.20	F14.20	Cocaine Use Disorder, Moderate or Severe
305.60	F14.10	Cocaine Use Disorder, Mild
305.70	F15.10	Amphetamine Use Disorder, Mild
304.40	F15.20	Amphetamine Use Disorder, Moderate or Severe
305.50	F11.10	Opioid Use Disorder, Mild
304.00	F11.20	Opioid Use Disorder, Moderate or Severe
305.90	F18.10	Inhalant Use Disorder, Mild
304.60	F18.20	Inhalant Use Disorder, Moderate or Severe
296.xx	F32.x	Major Depressive Disorder, Single Episode
296.xx	F33.x	Major Depressive Disorder, Recurrent Episode
301.83	F60.3	Borderline Personality Disorder
301.9	.9	Unspecified Personality Disorder

SELF-BLAME

BEHAVIORAL DEFINITIONS

1. Chronic and recurrent thoughts of blaming self for the sexual abuse/ trauma.
2. Feelings of inappropriate guilt and shame; viewing self as damaged goods.
3. Persistent feelings of being alone and isolated.
4. Chronic feelings of hopelessness, worthlessness, or inappropriate guilt.
5. Low self-esteem.
6. Avoids social relationships because of deep-seated sense of shame about self.

__. _____
_____
__. _____
_____
__. _____
_____

LONG-TERM GOALS

1. Decrease attribution of blame to self as having caused or having any responsibility for the abuse/assault.
2. Place responsibility for the offense on the offender.
3. Identify and restructure belief system and decrease primary identification with the abuse, with the abuse becoming a part, rather than the entirety, of personal life experiences.

4. Improve emotional functioning based on the abuse being only a part of history rather than a total focus of life.

5. Develop healthy cognitive patterns and beliefs leading to increased hopefulness, empowerment, and increased self-esteem.

__. _____
   _____

__. _____
   _____

__. _____
   _____

SHORT-TERM OBJECTIVES

1. Verbalize thoughts and feelings surrounding the sexual abuse. (1, 2, 3)

2. Eliminate self-blame statements when talking about the abuse, and place blame on the offender. (4, 5, 6)

THERAPEUTIC INTERVENTIONS

1. Explore the victim's incidents of sexual abuse victimization, allowing him/her to disclose only as much detail as he/she is comfortable with.

2. Monitor the victim's self-blame statements as he/she talks about the sexual abuse; gently highlight this self-blame when it occurs.

3. Assist the victim in identifying the themes of shame and guilt that occur in his/her daily thinking about the assault.

4. Have the victim practice verbalizations that assign blame to the offender for the sexual assault; use modeling to reframe self-blame statements.

3. Express feelings of powerlessness and anger surrounding the abuse experience. (7)

4. Verbalize an increased knowledge of how the perpetrator used manipulation before, during, and after the abuse to influence the attribution of the crime. (8)

5. Verbalize an understanding of the different forms that sexual abuse takes. (9)

6. Express acceptance of the fact that by placing responsibility on the offender, feelings of anger and rage may increase. (10, 11)

5. Assist the victim in identifying his/her cognitive distortions that underlie the self-blame (e.g., "I was probably too friendly"; "I should have resisted more"; or "I am a bad person").

6. Help the victim to put responsibility on the offender for the sexual trauma by assignment of reading *The Courage to Heal* (Bass and Davis).

7. Express empathy to the victim about his/her feelings of anger and powerlessness regarding the traumatic sexual abuse.

8. Teach the victim about manipulation and cognitive distortions used by sexual offenders in order to deny responsibility for the abuse (e.g., minimizing, blaming the victim, denial).

9. Clarify for the victim the different types of abuse and that sexual abuse does not always mean physical contact (e.g., exposing genitals, showing the victim pornography, masturbating in front of the victim).

10. Teach the victim that being angry with the perpetrator may be an essential part of the process of recovery and healing as blame is clearly placed on the offender.

11. Teach the victim specific strategies to deal with his/her anger toward the offender. (See the Anger Difficulties chapter in the Victim Issues part of this Planner.)

7. Read material that is informative regarding the feelings of self-blame and manipulation. (12)

12. Have the victim read material regarding anger and self-blame (e.g., *When Bad Things Happen to Good People* by Kushner and the *Surviving Childhood Sexual Abuse Workbook* by Ainscough and Toon).

8. Write a confrontational letter to the abuser to clarify that the abuser is responsible for the offense. (13)

13. Assign the victim to write a letter (unsent) to the offender regarding feelings about abuse; critique the letter about appropriately assigning blame to the offender for abuse/assault.

9. Process a victim clarification letter from the abuser in which the offender clearly accepts the blame for the sexual abuse. (14, 15, 16)

14. Evaluate the emotional stability of the victim to see if he/she is ready to read the victim clarification letter from the offender. (See the Denial chapter in the Offender Issues part of this Planner.)

15. Review the victim clarification letter from the offender before allowing the victim to read it to evaluate for manipulation, cognitive distortions, and denial.

16. Ask the victim read the victim clarification letter; process his/her feelings, evaluating for emotional stability and need for support.

10. Verbalize an understanding that while guilt may be a signal to evaluate a specific behavior, global shame about self as a person is destructive to self-esteem. (17, 18)

11. Identify distorted automatic thoughts that underlie shame in situations not related to the sexual abuse. (19)

12. Ask others for their views on when guilt and shame are warranted. (20)

13. Identify and replace dysfunctional thoughts about the abuse/assault that result in acceptance that the abuse was deserved or somehow a punishment for sin. (21, 22)

17. Assign the victim to read material regarding recovery from shame (e.g., *Healing the Shame That Binds You* by Bradshaw or *Shame* by Kaufman); process key concepts with him/her.

18. Obtain a detailed family history that examines the role of the family of origin in teaching the victim attitudes regarding guilt and shame.

19. Probe the victim's distorted automatic thoughts that trigger shame in different situations apart from the sexual abuse (e.g., when making mistakes, being assertive, asking for help); replace his/her distorted thoughts with positive, realistic self-talk.

20. Assign the victim to initiate three discussions with other people over a week regarding their views on the topic of when it is appropriate to feel guilt; process the insights that are gained from these discussions.

21. Ask the victim to keep a daily record of thoughts that are associated with shame and guilt, particularly noting those that are associated with deserving punishment and committing a sin.

22. Use logic and reality to challenge each dysfunctional assumption regarding having committed a sin or deserving punishment, replacing it with a realistic assumption.

14. Report improved self-esteem due to decreasing guilt and shame thoughts and increasing positive thoughts about self. (23, 24, 25)

23. Assist the victim in identifying and listing positive traits about himself/herself.

24. Use specific cognitive strategies to build self-esteem (e.g., ask the victim to express positive statements about himself/herself in front of a mirror daily; teach the victim to challenge negative self-talk).

25. Assign the victim to read *Feeling Good: The New Mood Therapy* (Burns) and to discuss with the therapist how thoughts impact feelings.

15. List reasons why the offender is responsible for the abuse/assault. (26)

26. Assist the victim in listing the reasons why the offender is solely responsible for the sexual abuse (e.g., use of force, use of position of power, victim was under the age of consent).

16. List the ways that the offender possessed power over the victim. (27, 28)

27. Discuss ways the offender had power over the victim (e.g., the offender was larger or stronger that the victim; the offender was in a position of authority over the victim; the offender was an adult, and the victim was a child).

28. Address issues of powerlessness and hopelessness regarding the abuse and how it impacts current life.

17. Describe the perceived and anticipated negative consequences of reporting the abuse to the authorities. (29)

18. Verbalize an understanding that the sexual arousal experienced during the abuse does not mean the abuse was desired. (30)

19. Verbalize a decrease in shame and guilt regarding experiencing sexual arousal as a natural consequence to genital stimulation, even during abuse. (31)

20. Identify how an abuser can manipulate an emotionally needy victim into initiating the abuse. (32)

21. Use art to express feelings about the abuse. (33)

29. Assist the victim in understanding the reasons victims don't tell about the abuse (e.g., fear of retaliation, fear of physical harm, fear of family breakup); compare these reasons with his/her experience.

30. Help the victim to understand that genital stimulation can cause sexual arousal during abuse in childhood, but that does not mean that he/she was responsible for the abuse or desired it.

31. Assist the victim in identifying his/her cognitive distortions that result in guilt feelings and shame about enjoying the attention or sexual arousal associated with the abuse (e.g., "It must have been my fault because my body was aroused"; "I could have fought back harder"; "There must have been something I could have done to stop it").

32. Assist the victim in understanding how low self-esteem and the need for attention or nurturance could be manipulated by distorted messages from the offender and lead to a victim seeking out or even inciting the abuse.

33. Use art (along with other creative and expressive methods) to encourage the victim to depict himself/herself being assertive with the abuser, reclaiming power, and assertively blaming the offender.

22. Verbalize an understanding that recovery from abuse/assault proceeds in stages, as in the grieving process for the loss of a loved one. (34, 35)

34. Teach the victim the stages of the grieving process, and point out that the process of recovering from sexual trauma is similar to the stages of recovering from the loss of a loved one (e.g., denial, bargaining, anger).

35. Assign the victim to read material on grief and recovery. (See *On Death and Dying* by Kubler-Ross, *When Bad Things Happen to Good People* by Kushner, or *Good Grief* by Westberg.)

23. Participate in dance, movement, music, or art therapy as a means of feeling freer, less anxious, self-conscious, and inhibited. (36)

36. Recommend that the victim become involved in supporting therapies (e.g., art, dance, music, and movement therapy).

24. List constructive strategies for dealing with the recurrence of distorted cognitions regarding guilt, shame, and attribution of blame for the abuse. (37, 38)

37. Help the victim to identify abuse as in the past, and restructure his/her belief system to help facilitate this.

38. Teach the victim that periodic recurrences of shame, guilt, and anger will recur and assist him/her in listing coping strategies to use at that time [e.g., repeating positive affirmations about himself/herself; reading a book about victimization, such as *The Courage to Heal* (Bass and Davis); attending a victim support group].

__. _____
_____
__. _____
_____
__. _____

__. _____
_____
__. _____
_____
__. _____

DIAGNOSTIC SUGGESTIONS:

ICD-9-CM	*ICD-10-CM*	*DSM-5* Disorder, Condition, or Problem
309.81	F43.10	Posttraumatic Stress Disorder
300.14	F44.81	Dissociative Identity Disorder
300.6	F48.1	Depersonalization/Derealization Disorder
300.15	F44.9	Unspecified Dissociative Disorder
300.15	F44.89	Other Specified Dissociative Disorder
309.0	F43.21	Adjustment Disorder, With Depressed Mood
995.53	T74.22XA	Child Sexual Abuse, Confirmed, Initial Encounter
995.53	T74.22XD	Child Sexual Abuse, Confirmed, Subsequent Encounter
995.83	T74.21XA	Spouse or Partner Violence, Sexual, Confirmed, Initial Encounter
995.83	T74.21XD	Spouse or Partner Violence, Sexual, Confirmed, Subsequent Encounter
995.83	T74.21XA	Adult Sexual Abuse by Nonspouse or Nonpartner, Confirmed, Initial Encounter
995.83	T74.21XD	Adult Sexual Abuse by Nonspouse or Nonpartner, Confirmed, Subsequent Encounter
995.54	T74.12XA	Child Physical Abuse, Confirmed, Initial Encounter
995.54	T74.12XD	Child Physical Abuse, Confirmed, Subsequent Encounter
V61.12	Z69.12	Encounter for Mental Health Services for Perpetrator of Spouse or Partner Violence, Physical
V62.83	Z69.82	Encounter for Mental Health Services for Perpetrator of Nonspousal Adult Abuse
308.3	F43.0	Acute Stress Disorder
303.90	F10.20	Alcohol Use Disorder, Moderate or Severe
305.00	F10.10	Alcohol Use Disorder, Mild
304.30	F12.20	Cannabis Use Disorder, Moderate or Severe
305.20	F12.10	Cannabis Use Disorder, Mild
304.20	F14.20	Cocaine Use Disorder, Moderate or Severe
305.60	F14.10	Cocaine Use Disorder, Mild
305.70	F15.10	Amphetamine Use Disorder, Mild
304.40	F15.20	Amphetamine Use Disorder, Moderate or Severe
305.50	F11.10	Opioid Use Disorder, Mild
304.00	F11.20	Opioid Use Disorder, Moderate or Severe
305.90	F18.10	Inhalant Use Disorder, Mild
304.60	F18.20	Inhalant Use Disorder, Moderate or Severe
296.xx	F32.x	Major Depressive Disorder, Single Episode
296.xx	F33.x	Major Depressive Disorder, Recurrent Episode
301.83	F60.3	Borderline Personality Disorder
301.9	F60.9	Unspecified Personality Disorder

SELF-INJURY

BEHAVIORAL DEFINITIONS

1. Consistent pattern of burning, cutting, scraping flesh, hitting, or bruising self.
2. Uses self-injury to reduce negative affect.
3. Repeated pattern of self-mutilation despite negative physical consequences.
4. Extreme emotional reactivity (e.g., anger, anxiety, or depression) under minor stress that usually does not last more than a few hours to a few days.
5. Chronic feelings of emptiness and boredom.
6. A pattern of intense, chaotic interpersonal relationships.
7. Easily feels that others are treating him/her unfairly or that they can't be trusted.
8. Marked identity disturbance.
9. Becomes very anxious with any hint of perceived abandonment in a relationship.

__. _____
   _____

__. _____
   _____

__. _____
   _____

LONG-TERM GOALS

1. Break the cycle of self-abuse.
2. Decrease the frequency of urges to engage in self-mutilation.

3. Develop adaptive methods to reduce high levels of negative affect rather than using self-damaging behavior.
4. Identify the triggers for self-harm, and develop a safety plan.

__. _____
    _____

__. _____
    _____

__. _____
    _____

SHORT-TERM OBJECTIVES

1. Describe details of when and how self-injury first began. (1, 2)

2. Rate the intensity of the urge to self-injure by using a 10-point Likert scale, noting how the intensity rises and falls during the day. (3)

3. Identify high-risk times and circumstances when the urge to self-injure is greatest. (4, 5)

THERAPEUTIC INTERVENTIONS

1. Explore with the victim the history of his/her self-injury behavior.

2. Ask the victim to make a list of all the ways that he/she has self-injured, including less obvious methods (e.g., picking at scabs or pulling hair out).

3. Show the victim how to use a journal or log book to record the intensity of the urge to self-injure, and practice rating the urge in session using a 10-point Likert scale with defined anchor points.

4. Review the victim's self-injury journal to identify times when the urge to self-injure is high, and determine if it relates to meals, sleep deprivation, time of day, or other factors.

4. Identify the negative conse-
    quences of self-injury. (6)

5. Get feedback from significant
    others regarding their feelings
    and thoughts about the self-
    injury behavior. (7)

6. Identify distorted thoughts as-
    sociated with the cycle of self-
    abuse, and correct thinking
    errors. (8, 9, 10)

5. Review the victim's self-injury
    journal to identify triggers of
    self-injury (e.g., thoughts of
    being bad, need to be in con-
    trol, perfectionism, turning
    anger inward, feelings of
    worthlessness, self-hatred,
    abandonment).

6. Assign the victim to make a
    list of all the ways self-injury
    has made a negative impact on
    his/her life (e.g., social, medi-
    cal, occupational, emotional);
    process the list.

7. Assign the victim the task of
    asking significant others how
    they feel about his/her self-
    injury; process these responses
    in session.

8. Assist the victim in identifying
    his/her thoughts that precede
    self-injury behavior, and chal-
    lenge these thoughts.

9. Examine the victim's distorted
    cognitions that accompany
    self-injury (e.g., "It's the only
    way I can feel better; I have no
    idea why I cut myself . . . I
    can't control it"); teach adap-
    tive, positive thoughts to re-
    place distortions.

10. Ask the victim to list his/her
    fears of imagined conse-
    quences (e.g., fear of being
    overwhelmed by emotions,
    fear of being out of control,
    fear of having no way to ex-
    press himself/herself) if he/she
    stops self-injuring; process this
    list in session.

7. Describe experiences of sexual and other abuse and the feelings associated with these painful memories. (11, 12)

8. Accurately identify feelings that precede or lead to the urge to self-injure. (12, 13, 14)

9. List instances where self-injury has functioned to distract from emotionally disturbing memories of abuse. (11, 15)

11. Help the victim to understand how self-injury may serve the purpose of distracting him/her from painful memories of abuse by exploring abuse memories in session and verbalizing associated feelings.

12. Use modeling and role play to teach the victim appropriate ways to express his/her feelings, the expression of which may have been punished in childhood.

12. Use modeling and role play to teach the victim appropriate ways to express his/her feelings, the expression of which may have been punished in childhood.

13. Give the victim a printed sheet of words that describe many feelings to help him/her identify feelings (see *Skills Training for Children with Behavior Disorders* by Bloomquist); practice using this cue sheet in session.

14. Help the victim to learn to outline the thoughts and feelings that precede a self-injury incident, and assign him/her to record these in a self-injury journal.

11. Help the victim to understand how self-injury may serve the purpose of distracting him/her from painful memories of abuse by exploring abuse memories in session and verbalizing associated feelings.

10. Implement adaptive techniques to cope with uncomfortable negative feelings that are associated with painful experiences. (16, 17)

11. Gain information about self-injury by reading books or Internet sources. (18)

15. Help the victim to understand that self-injury may serve the purpose of distracting him/her from painful memories of abuse by identifying specific abuse stimuli that increase negative affect (e.g., the smell of beer, watching a violent television program, experiencing feelings of sexual arousal).

16. Teach the victim ways to cope with uncomfortable feelings other than self-injury (e.g., practicing assertive behaviors, implementing relaxation techniques).

17. Teach the victim alternative methods to stop his/her intrusive memories and flashbacks, and to refocus on the present (e.g., deep breathing techniques, deep muscle relaxation, positive memory insertion, thought-stopping techniques).

18. Refer the victim to information in books on self-injury (e.g., *Women Who Hurt Themselves: A Book of Hope and Understanding* by Miller; *Bodily Harm: The Breakthrough Healing Program for Self-Injurers* by Contario, Lader, and Kingson; *Understanding Self-Injury: A Workbook for Adults* by Trautman and Connors) and Internet self-injury informational message boards or web sites (e.g., www.safe-alternatives.com or www.healthyplace.com).

12. Use specific behavioral and cognitive techniques that decrease the urge to self-injure. (19, 20, 21, 22)

19. Assist the victim in listing 10 alternatives to self-injury when the urge is high (e.g., call a support person and talk about the urge; take a warm bath; draw a picture of current feelings using many vivid colors).

20. Identify and challenge the victim's thoughts that fuel escalation of self-injury urges, and teach him/her to focus instead on calm-ing thoughts and deep breathing.

21. Suggest that the victim implement constructive activities as substitute actions for self-injury (e.g., scrubbing the floor with a brush, sweeping the sidewalk, or walking very fast).

22. Assist the victim in making a list of actions to use specifically when angry or frustrated, that in some way substitute for the action of self-injury (e.g., hitting a punching bag, drawing on a piece of paper with a red marker, tearing paper into little pieces, stomping and yelling, throwing nonbreakable objects at a brick wall).

13. Verbalize positive statements about self when observing even small decreases in self-injury behavior. (23)

23. Encourage the victim to verbalize positive statements about himself/herself even when small gains are made (e.g., not self-injuring for 24 hours).

14. List the benefits of stopping self-injury. (24)

24. Assist the victim in listing the positive aspects of stopping self-injury (e.g., decreased risk for infection, increased self-esteem, decreased conflict with significant others because of self-inflicted injuries).

15. When experiencing urges to self-injure, practice delay techniques. (25, 26)

16. Use sensory stimulation techniques to decrease the desire to self-injure. (27)

17. Develop a written plan of increasing social contacts to help decrease the urge to self-injure. (28, 29, 30)

18. Develop a written procedure regarding how to get appropriate medical care for self-injury wounds. (31)

25. Assign the victim to use a delay task using cognitive-behavioral techniques (e.g., thought stopping or reframing) when experiencing an urge to self-injure.

26. Have the victim set a few-minute time limit using an alarm clock to delay self-injury and note how the intensity of the urge changes.

27. Assist the victim in listing 10 distracting things to do that are intensely stimulating to one of the senses instead of engaging in self-injury (e.g., chewing on ice, smelling different strong spices such as ginger or mint, listening to loud music, taking a cold shower).

28. Assist the victim in listing a support network of people who know about the self-injury and who will be supportive when the urge to self-injure is strong.

29. Reinforce and encourage the victim to have emotional needs met by more direct means of communication rather than using self-injury; use role playing and modeling to teach him/her how to make direct requests to significant others.

30. Assign the victim to tell someone about the self-injury who previously was unaware of it; process the feelings in session.

31. Help the victim to develop a plan to access medical care through an emergency room, urgent care center, or primary

19. Write a letter to the physician outlining the safety plan and self-care contract. (32, 33)

20. List ways to cope with scars from self-injury. (34, 35)

21. Consult with a psychiatrist for a medication evaluation, and comply with the recommendations. (36)

22. Take medications as prescribed, and report any side effects to appropriate professionals. (37)

care physician, so that he/she can have wounds treated with dignity and in a supportive environment.

32. Develop a contract with the victim that he/she will seek medical attention within a specific time limit (as recommended by the physician) if he/she self-injures.

33. Ask the victim to write a letter regarding a safety plan and self-care contract to medical professionals; review this letter in session.

34. Assist the victim in listing 10 ways to decrease anxiety and shame regarding scars from self-injury (e.g., consulting with a plastic surgeon, using a concealing makeup such as Dermablend, wearing long sleeves).

35. Teach the victim alternative assertive and/or humorous ways to respond to people who ask about the self-injury scars (e.g., "I'd rather not talk about it"; "What scars?").

36. Refer the victim for a medication evaluation to remediate mood instability or anxiety and to help decrease his/her self-injury urge.

37. Monitor medication compliance, side effects, and effectiveness. Confer with the physician regularly.

23. Contract with the therapist to agree to an evaluation for inpatient hospitalization if the urge to self-injure becomes uncontrollable. (38)

24. Participating as a team member, agree to cooperate with medical and psychiatric professionals in order to promote a decrease in self-injury. (39)

__. _____
_____

__. _____
_____

__. _____
_____

38. Develop a specific written plan for hospitalization if the threat of self-injury is severe, and ask the victim to sign an agreement to the plan.

39. Manage self-injury with a team, including, if possible, a psychiatrist, a primary care physician, a group therapist and individual therapist, and the victim.

__. _____
_____

__. _____
_____

__. _____
_____

DIAGNOSTIC SUGGESTIONS:

ICD-9-CM	_ICD-10-CM_	_DSM-5_ Disorder, Condition, or Problem
300.4	F34.1	Persistent Depressive Disorder
296.xx	F32.x	Major Depressive Disorder, Single Episode
296.xx	F33.x	Major Depressive Disorder, Recurrent Episode
309.81	F43.10	Posttraumatic Stress Disorder
301.83	F60.3	Borderline Personality Disorder
300.14	F44.81	Dissociative Identity Disorder
300.15	F44.89	Other Specified Dissociative Disorder
300.15	F44.9	Unspecified Dissociative Disorder
_____	_____	_____
_____	_____	_____

SOCIAL WITHDRAWAL

BEHAVIORAL DEFINITIONS

1. Avoidance of activities with others because of anxiety, fear, shame, mistrust, or feelings of inadequacy.
2. Excessive and persistent worry about interacting with others in a social environment.
3. Overall pattern of social anxiety, shyness, or timidity that presents itself in most social situations.
4. Isolation or involvement in solitary activities during most waking hours.
5. Symptoms of hypervigilance, such as being constantly on edge when with people.
6. Strong feelings of panic or fear, such as increased heart rate, sweating, muscle tension, and shakiness when faced with social interactions.
7. Abuse of alcohol or chemicals to help avoid or ease the anxiety of becoming involved in social situations.

__. _____
   _____
   _____
__. _____
   _____
   _____
__. _____
   _____

LONG-TERM GOALS

1. Interact socially without excessive fear or anxiety.
2. Develop the essential social skills that will enhance the quality of a relationship life.
3. Develop the ability to form relationships and to attend group functions that will enhance sexual trauma recovery support system.

4. Reach a healthy personal balance between solitary time and interpersonal interaction with others.
5. Terminate the use of alcohol or chemicals to relieve social anxiety and implement constructive coping behaviors.

__. _____
_____
__. _____
_____
__. _____
_____

SHORT-TERM OBJECTIVES

THERAPEUTIC INTERVENTIONS

1. Identify socially avoidant behaviors that are engaged in as the result of shame, anxiety, fear, low self-esteem, and so forth. (1, 2)

1. Assist the victim in coming to the realization that he/she is withdrawn from others because of negative affect (e.g., fear, anxiety, guilt, or shame) and distorted cognitions that precipitate those feelings.

2. Engage in building rapport by expressing empathy for the victim's feelings of isolation and anxiety.

2. Identify the connection between family-of-origin experiences and current interpersonal functioning. (3)

3. Probe the victim's childhood experiences of criticism, perfectionism, or patterns of family social avoidance or anxiety that would fos-ter his/her current social withdrawal.

3. Identify the impact that the sexual abuse/trauma has had on social interactions. (4)

4. Ask the victim to describe the change in himself/ herself since the sexual assault, clarifying how sexual abuse influenced self-image and how that impacts socializing with others.

4. Replace distorted, negative cognitions related to sexual abuse with more realistic, positive self-talk. (5, 6)

5. Assist the victim in identifying internal thought processes that impact self-esteem, listing negative thoughts about himself/herself that originated with the sexual abuse.

6. Apply logical reasoning to replace each of the victim's distorted assumptions about himself/herself with more realistic, positive self-talk.

5. Comply with recommendations for psychological testing. (7)

7. Refer for or administer psychological testing to assess social anxiety, general anxiety, self-esteem, and/or depression [e.g., Leibowitz Social Anxiety Scale, Social Phobia Inventory, Beck Depression Inventory (BDI), or Minnesota Multiphasic Personality Inventory—2 (MMPI-2)]; give feedback of results and target areas for intervention.

6. Cooperate with and complete a psychiatric evaluation. (8)

8. Refer the victim to a psychiatrist for a psychotropic medication evaluation.

7. Take medication as ordered on a consistent basis, reporting effectiveness and any side effects to the physician. (9)

9. Monitor the victim's medication effectiveness and side effects, and encourage compliance with the prescription.

8. Identify situations that lead to social discomfort by a daily journal notation of cognitions and feelings. (6, 10, 11)

6. Apply logical reasoning to replace each of the victim's distorted assumptions about himself/herself with more realistic, positive self-talk.

10. Ask the victim to keep a daily feelings journal in which he/she documents situations that result in fear, shame, anxiety, and withdrawal from socializing.

11. Challenge the victim's distorted cognitions that lead to feelings of shame, hopelessness, and inferiority by probing with questions designed to have the victim produce evidence of the anxiety and logical reasons for it being present. (See *Anxiety Disorders and Phobias* by Beck and Emery.)

9. Report an increased understanding of how distorted cognitions regarding assignment of blame to the victim lead to negative affect and low self-esteem. (12, 13)

12. Assign the victim to read *The Courage to Heal* (Bass and Davis), and process key ideas regarding his/her tendency to blame himself/herself.

13. Explore the victim's tendency to blame himself/herself for the sexual assault; replace the cognitive distortions that precipitate that feeling of self-blame.

10. Use relaxation methods to decrease anxiety and improve ability to calm self in social situations. (14)

14. Teach the victim relaxation methods used to cope with anxiety associated with social interaction (e.g., progressive muscle relaxation, deep breathing techniques, self-hypnosis, positive guided imagery).

11. Replace the cognitive distortions used to deny needs for interpersonal interaction. (15)

15. Process with the victim his/her fears of intimacy, and his/her anxiety about close relationships to others; correct cognitive distortions that feed this fear. (See the Trust Impairment chapter in the Victim Issues part of this Planner.)

12. Report an increase in the use of assertiveness skills. (16, 17)

16. Use role playing and modeling to teach the victim about the difference between aggressive, passive, and assertive behavior,

13. Use desensitization techniques to overcome any persistent and unreasonable fear of social situations that leads to an intense anxiety reaction and subsequent social avoidance. (18)

14. Verbalize an understanding that the feelings of social anxiety result from irrational self-talk and that the phobic avoidance of social situations functions as an escape from feeling out of control and uncomfortable. (19, 20)

15. Verbalize an increased feeling of confidence in and approval of self. (21, 22)

and how to use assertiveness to solve problems in relationships (e.g., how to say no to a request from another person, how to discuss feelings with friends, how to discuss anger).

17. Assign the victim to attend assertiveness training classes as a way of improving social skills.

18. Assist the victim in developing an exposure hierarchy to be used in vivo to desensitize himself/herself to anxiety-producing stimuli; ask him/her to track progress by keeping a daily journal.

19. Assign the victim to read books on overcoming social anxiety (e.g., *Mastery of Your Anxiety and Panic* by Barlow and Craske or *Dying of Embarrassment: Help for Social Anxiety and Phobia* by Carmin, Pollard, and Flynn); process key concepts.

20. Teach the victim that feelings of social anxiety result from irrational self-talk and that the anxiety feelings lead to avoidance or escape behaviors.

21. Assist the victim in establishing a goal to reduce the power that anxiety has over his/her life by learning how to reduce his/her fear of social disapproval by reducing his/her disapproval of himself/herself.

22. Encourage the victim to verbalize positive beliefs about himself/herself, practicing once daily while looking in the mirror.

16. Report an increased tolerance for accepting self when making small mistakes in front of others. (23, 24, 25, 26, 27)

23. Have the victim keep a daily journal and plot thoughts, occurrences, and level of anxiety at regular intervals on a 10-point Likert scale. Discuss antecedent cognitions (e.g., perfectionism) that lead to an increase in anxiety levels in social situations.

24. Encourage the victim to record the small mistakes that he/she makes on a daily basis and monitor the cognitions that occur as a result of each mistake.

25. Support the victim when he/she reports increased tolerance for himself/herself when he/she makes mistakes.

26. Explore more adaptive cognitions (e.g., "Everybody makes mistakes"; "It's okay to make mistakes"; "I'm doing fine") to employ as self-talk in social situations when faced with anxiety symptoms (e.g., rapid heart rate, increased sweating, urge to run out of the room), based in perfectionism.

27. Use paradoxical strategy and assign the victim to deliberately make a small mistake in a social situation (e.g., wear a slightly mismatching outfit to a social function; exit a crowded row in a theater during a movie; accidentally spill water on himself/herself at a social function); process these feelings with him/her, and identify negative cognitions about himself/herself.

17. Increase social interactions with others who have survived sexual abuse/trauma. (28)

18. Increase social group activities to at least two per week. (29, 30)

19. Attend a sexual abuse survivors group. (31)

20. Implement the use of guided visualization of success in social situations. (32)

21. Participate in a weekend activity with other people. (33)

28. Encourage and support the victim to have contact with other supportive survivors of sexual trauma (e.g., support meetings, group therapy, Internet message boards).

29. Ask the victim to list activities in which he/she would enjoy engaging that included others (e.g., sports, hobbies, religious worship); solicit a commitment from him/her to engage in two such activities per week.

30. Review the victim's experience with social activity participation; reinforce success, and redirect to reduce anxiety using behavioral and cognitive techniques.

31. Refer the victim to interpersonal groups that could offer support for healing from abuse/trauma (e.g., Survivors of Incest Anonymous, Incest Survivors Anonymous, Families United).

32. Lead the victim in a guided visualization in which he/she views himself/herself as being successful in social situations, and ask him/her to practice this visualization daily.

33. Assign the victim to join others in a group activity that lasts for one or two days (e.g., a camping trip organized by the Sierra Club, a weekend trip to visit a museum, a weekend CPR class); process feelings and thoughts about being with others.

22. Develop a life plan that includes a commitment to meeting social needs balanced with time alone. (34, 35)

34. Explore with the victim balancing social and individual time in a way that would result in a satisfying, fulfilled life. Reinforce the victim for interacting with others even when anxiety accompanies socialization.

35. Ask the victim to verbalize a commitment to a lifelong plan of increasing social confidence and comfort, and decreasing social anxiety.

__. _____
_____

__. _____
_____

__. _____
_____

__. _____
_____

__. _____
_____

__. _____
_____

DIAGNOSTIC SUGGESTIONS:

ICD-9-CM	_ICD-10-CM_	_DSM-5_ Disorder, Condition, or Problem
300.23	F40.10	Social Anxiety Disorder (Social Phobia)
300.4	F34.1	Persistent Depressive Disorder
296.xx	F32.x	Major Depressive Disorder, Single Episode
296.xx	F33.x	Major Depressive Disorder, Recurrent Episode
300.22	F40.00	Agoraphobia
300.01	F41.0	Panic Disorder
309.81	F43.10	Posttraumatic Stress Disorder
301.82	F60.6	Avoidant Personality Disorder
301.0	F60.0	Paranoid Personality Disorder
_____	_____	_____
_____	_____	_____

TRUST IMPAIRMENT

BEHAVIORAL DEFINITIONS

1. Consistent distrust of others.
2. Expectation of being exploited or harmed by others.
3. Expectation of being shunned by others because of shame regarding the sexual trauma.
4. Tends to be socially and emotionally isolated out of fear of being hurt.
5. Avoidance of emotional intimacy with others leads to a pattern of superficial relationships.
6. Lacks a positive support network.
7. Excessive involvement in activities (e.g., work, hobbies) that allows for avoidance of closeness with others.
8. Difficulties in judging the trustworthiness of others.

__. _____

_____

__. _____

_____

__. _____

_____

LONG-TERM GOALS

1. Interact with others with reduced vigilance, decreased defensiveness, and increased trust.
2. Develop emotionally supportive close friends.
3. Increase social interaction with trustworthy others.
4. Gradually take the risk of building an intimate relationship with a trustworthy partner.

5. Develop a cognitive strategy for judging others' and own behavior for impediments to intimacy such as untrustworthy behaviors.

—. _____

_____

—. _____

_____

—. _____

_____

SHORT-TERM OBJECTIVES

1. Describe the history of difficulties experienced with respect to trust and the impact on relationships. (1, 2, 3)

2. Identify fears that lead to social and emotional isolation. (4)

3. Verbalize an increased awareness of feelings of shame and the role that shame plays in relationships. (5, 6)

THERAPEUTIC INTERVENTIONS

1. Express empathy for the victim's feelings of fear and anxiety regarding trusting others.

2. Probe family-of-origin history for sources of difficulties with intimacy and negative learned attitudes about relationships.

3. Explore how the victim's reasons for avoiding intimacy are related to the sexual abuse.

4. Assist the victim in identifying his/her fears that lead to avoidance of being close to others (e.g., fear of being rejected, fear that he/she is unworthy of love, fear of his/her own anger).

5. Explore the victim's feelings of shame and how shame plays a role in keeping him/her isolated from others.

6. Assign the victim to read books on shame recovery (e.g., *Healing the Shame That Binds You* by Bradshaw and *Facing Shame* by Fossum and Mason); process key issues, particularly those related to sexual abuse.

4. Identify and replace distorted thoughts that lead to distancing self from people. (7, 8)

5. Participate in art or drama techniques to resolve and heal past relationship traumas. (9, 10)

6. Identify ways in which the offender betrayed trust. (11, 12)

7. Assist the victim in identifying distorted self-talk messages that lead to fear and avoidance of others (e.g., "I feel so dirty"; "They think I'm responsible for the sexual activity"; or "Everyone is out to take advantage of me").

8. Assist the victim in replacing dysfunctional thoughts with rational, positive cognitive messages (e.g., "I am a good person"; "No one who truly loves me blames me for being a victim"; "Many people can be gradually trusted").

9. Use art to help the victim decrease his/her affective response of fear of rejection because of his/her shame related to the abuse. Instruct the victim to produce an abstract expression of his/her emotions through the use of crayons, paints, or collage.

10. Use drama therapy to play out worst possible scenarios regarding rejection from others, feelings of shame, and subsequent recovery.

11. Assist the victim in seeing how the offender betrayed his/her trust and did not have integrity.

7. Terminate verbalizations of attribution of blame to self as having caused the abuse and give responsibility for the offense to the offender. (13)

8. List the indicators of trustworthiness in a relationship. (14)

9. Identify how others and self measure up to indicators of trustworthiness. (15, 16)

10. Identify and implement the basic skills necessary to facilitate maintenance of relationships. (17)

12. Use drama techniques in group therapy to help the victim process feelings regarding betrayal in a confrontation with the offender about trust; direct him/her to explore different ways of confrontation and to increase his/her understanding of the betrayal.

13. Consistently teach the victim that the offender is responsible for the sexual abuse; confront his/her self-attributions of blame, and reinforce his/her placing blame directly on the offender.

14. Have the victim list the aspects of integrity and trustworthiness (e.g., kindness, interest in others' welfare, honesty, keeping commitments, accepting responsibility) that he/she desires in a relationship.

15. Have the victim list current significant others and describe how they meet or fail the standards of trustworthiness that he/she has identified.

16. Discuss with the victim how he/she meets or fails his/her own standards of trustworthiness.

17. Teach the victim or refer him/her to a social skills group addressing the essential social skills that will enhance the quality of relationships. (See the Social Withdrawal chapter in the Victim Issues part of this Planner.)

11. Cooperate with a referral to a physician to evaluate the need for psychotropic medication. (18)

12. Verbalize an increase in the desire for and pleasure in physical touch by setting clear and appropriate boundaries with a consensual sexual partner. (19, 20)

13. Participate in volunteer activities, and verbalize fears that are generated by social contact. (21)

14. Practice skills that encourage intimate attachments in long-term relationships. (22)

18. Make a referral to a physician to evaluate the victim for medication to remediate mood instability, and decrease anxiety, panic attacks, and/or depression.

19. Explore and define with the victim what kind of touch is acceptable, ranging from a handshake at a social event to intercourse in a consensual, supportive sexual relationship.

20. Encourage the victim to verbalize his/her physical sensitivities to his/her sexual partner by giving clear information about boundaries regarding the type of touch to avoid in order to not exacerbate PTSD or anxiety symptoms.

21. Assign the victim to choose and commit to minimal regular attendance at volunteer work in a nonthreatening environment (e.g., nursing home, soup kitchen, church-related activity); explore fears regarding relating to others, anxiety about others seeking to touch, or fears of rejection).

22. Teach the victim behaviors that increase intimacy (e.g., honesty, expressing and resolving anger, sharing attraction and other positive feelings, frequent eye contact), and explore which to use with safe people.

15. Keep a daily log of social interactions. (23)

16. Verbalize feelings in an appropriate manner with others daily. (24)

17. Verbalize a desire for positive intimate relationships. (25)

18. List goals for improved social interactions. (26)

23. Assign the victim to keep a journal of his/her taking mild social interaction risks one time per day; discuss his/her thoughts, feelings, and behavior.

24. Encourage the victim to share his/her feelings on a regular basis with others who meet his/her standards of trustworthiness in order to decrease anxiety about expressing feelings and improving intimacy skills.

25. Reinforce the victim's verbal expressions of a desire for closeness in relationships.

26. Encourage the victim to commit to positive goals regarding relationships (e.g., seek friends who are trustworthy, increase integrity in all relationships, give and seek emotional support from others, enter relationships based on personal moral values).

__. _____
   _____
__. _____
   _____
__. _____
   _____

__. _____
   _____
__. _____
   _____
__. _____
   _____

DIAGNOSTIC SUGGESTIONS:

ICD-9-CM	_ICD-10-CM_	_DSM-5_ Disorder, Condition, or Problem
309.81	F43.10	Posttraumatic Stress Disorder
296.xx	F32.x	Major Depressive Disorder, Single Episode
296.xx	F33.x	Major Depressive Disorder, Recurrent Episode
300.4	F34.1	Persistent Depressive Disorder
300.01	F41.0	Panic Disorder
300.22	F40.00	Agoraphobia
300.02	F41.1	Generalized Anxiety Disorder
300.09	F41.8	Other Specified Anxiety Disorder
300.00	F41.9	Unspecified Anxiety Disorder
301.83	F60.3	Borderline Personality Disorder
301.82	F60.6	Avoidant Personality Disorder
_____	_____	_____
_____	_____	_____

Part 2

OFFENDER ISSUES

ANGER DIFFICULTIES

BEHAVIORAL DEFINITIONS

1. History of initiating physically assaultive or coercive sexual contacts.
2. Lack of socially adaptive assertiveness skills with other adults.
3. Anger is experienced as a precursor to sexual offenses.
4. Unexpected and unpredictable feelings of rage.
5. History of explosive aggressive outbursts that are out of proportion to precipitating stressors leading to assaultive acts or destruction of property.
6. Overreactions of hostility to insignificant irritants.
7. Use of verbally abusive language.
8. Body language or tense muscles (e.g., clenched fist or jaw, glaring looks, or refusal to make eye contact).
9. Use of passive-aggressive patterns (e.g., social withdrawal due to anger, lack of complete or timely compliance in following directions or rules, complaining about authority figures behind their backs, or nonparticipation in meeting expected behavioral norms).

__. _____
   _____
__. _____
   _____
__. _____
   _____

LONG-TERM GOALS

1. Develop effective anger management strategies that will interrupt the sexual assault cycle.
2. Learn the assertiveness skills necessary to establish and maintain social relationships with appropriate adult partners, especially with respect to dealing with conflict.
3. Decrease overall intensity and frequency of angry feelings, and increase ability to recognize and appropriately express angry feelings as they occur.
4. Develop an awareness of current angry behaviors, clarifying origins of and alternatives to aggression, passive-aggressive behaviors, or suppression of anger.
5. Come to an awareness and acceptance of angry feelings while developing better behavioral control and more serenity.

__. _____
   _____
__. _____
   _____
__. _____
   _____

SHORT-TERM OBJECTIVES	THERAPEUTIC INTERVENTIONS
1. Verbally acknowledge experiencing feelings of anger. (1, 2)	1. Assist the offender in coming to the realization that he/she is angry by asking him/her to explore and label his/her feelings that surround his/her perceptions of being victimized, particularly by the legal system.
	2. Assign the offender to read the book *Of Course You're Angry* (Rosellini and Worden) or *The Angry Book* (Rubin).

2. Identify targets of and causes for anger in daily life. (2, 3, 4)

3. Verbalize an increased awareness of anger expression patterns. (5, 6)

4. Identify how significant others in childhood have modeled ways to handle anger. (7)

5. Identify the pain and hurt of past or current life that fuels ongoing anger. (8, 9)

2. Assign the offender to read the book *Of Course You're Angry* (Rosellini and Worden) or *The Angry Book* (Rubin).

3. Ask the offender to keep a daily journal that documents actions, environmental events, or internal thoughts that cause anger, frustration, or irritation.

4. Assign the offender to write a list of targets of and causes for anger; process this list in session.

5. Gently confront the offender about the transfer of angry feelings toward the therapist, either directly or indirectly, such as indicated by missed appointments, critical comments, or angry outbursts.

6. Refer the offender to an anger management class or group.

7. Explore family-of-origin rules regarding anger expression, and use a genogram to identify how significant others in childhood (e.g., parents, caretakers, siblings, teachers) expressed angry feelings.

8. Assign the offender to list the experiences of life that have hurt and led to anger.

9. Empathize with and clarify the offender's feelings of hurt and anger tied to traumas of the past.

6. Verbalize feelings of anger in a controlled, assertive way. (10, 11, 12, 13)

10. Teach the offender assertiveness skills, or assign him/her assertiveness training classes.

11. Process the offender's angry feelings or angry outbursts that have recently occurred, and review alternative behaviors that are available (e.g., taking a time-out, using deep breathing and relaxation techniques, speaking assertively but not aggressively, sharing feelings in writing or with a friend to diffuse anger).

12. Use role-playing techniques to assist the offender in developing non-self-defeating ways of handling angry feelings (e.g., assertive use of "I" messages).

13. Assign a specific verbal or written exercise addressing anger management (e.g., *Dr. Weisinger's Anger Work Out Book* by Weisinger or *Skills Training Manual for Treating Borderline Personality Disorder* by Linehan); process the exercise with the offender.

7. Use relaxation techniques to cope with angry feelings. (14)

14. Teach the offender relaxation techniques (e.g., deep breathing, positive guided imagery, deep muscle relaxation) to cope with initial response to angry feelings when they occur.

8. Verbalize an increased awareness of how maladaptive ways
of expressing angry feelings
have had a negative impact on
self and others. (15, 16)

9. Identify the physical manifestations of anger, aggression, or
violence. (11, 17, 18)

15. Ask the offender to list ways
that the maladaptive expression of anger had resulted in
negative consequences for
himself/herself and others, including sexual offense; process
the list of consequences.

16. Expand the offender's awareness of the negative effects
that perpetually feeling angry
has on his/her body and spirit.

11. Process the offender's angry
feelings or angry outbursts
that have recently occurred,
and review alternative behaviors that are available (e.g.,
taking a time-out, using deep
breathing and relaxation techniques, speaking assertively
but not aggressively, sharing
feelings in writing or with a
friend to diffuse anger).

17. Encourage the offender to observe and label angry feelings
while describing specific body
sensations that are associated
with the anger.

18. Review the offender's violent
expressions of anger and the
negative consequences for
himself/herself and others
(e.g., personal shame, distrust
and fear from others, legal
conflicts, injuries, loss of freedom, financial loss).

10. Report an increased awareness of anger triggers and the ability to react in a nonaggressive manner. (3, 19, 20)

11. Write an angry letter to the target of anger, and process this letter with the therapist. (21, 22)

12. Describe how a personal pattern of anger relates to a pattern of initiating sexual assault through distorted self-talk. (23)

3. Ask the offender to keep a daily journal that documents actions, environmental events, or internal thoughts that cause anger, frustration, or irritation.

19. Assist the offender in developing the ability to recognize his/her triggers that lead to angry outbursts.

20. Help the offender to develop emotional regulation skills, viewing anger as a wave that comes and goes, and encourage a willingness to feel anger. (See *Skills Training Manual for Treating Borderline Personality Disorder* by Linehan.)

21. Ask the offender to write an angry letter to his/her own sexual perpetrator, or whomever, focusing on the reasons for his/her anger toward that person. Process the letter in session.

22. Encourage the offender to express and release (while in session) feelings of anger, rage, and violent fantasies or plots for revenge; help the offender to develop alternative strategies of coping with anger.

23. Assist the offender in listing cognitive distortions that he/she uses when angry and how that contributes to the assault cycle.

13. Describe the role that anger played in the specific sexual offense(s). (24)

14. Verbalize accurately how the victim must have felt in response to the offender's anger. (25, 26)

15. Verbalize an acceptance of responsibility for the sexual abuse without assigning blame to the victim. (27, 28)

16. List the ways that anger can be communicated indirectly to intimidate others. (29, 30)

24. Assign the offender to write out a complete description of his/her sexual assault(s), identifying his/her feelings leading up to the offense.

25. Using role-playing techniques, ask the offender to assume the role of the victim and to verbalize the fear and confusion that results from being the target of the offender's anger or rage.

26. Explore the offender's own painful and fear-filled memories related to childhood traumas when he/she was the target of or witnessed another's rage.

27. Explore the offender's willingness to accept responsibility for the sexual assault without placing any blame on the victim or any others.

28. Consistently reinforce the offender's statements that place responsibility for the abuse on himself/herself, not the victim.

29. Help the offender explore body language factors (e.g., eye contact, voice tone, or posture) that communicate threat to another.

30. Assist the offender in choosing a support person in his/her environment to cue him/her when he/she is displaying behaviors associated with aggression or intimidation.

17. Identify instances in which anger has been used to manipulate vulnerable individuals. (31)

18. Describe own childhood feelings when confronted by anger of the significant parent figure who may have modeled uncontrollable anger. (26, 32, 33)

19. Report an understanding of the right to be and the need for being assertive. (34, 35, 36, 37)

31. Assist the offender in reviewing occasions when he/she has used anger to manipulate someone.

26. Explore the offender's own painful and fear-filled memories related to childhood traumas when he/she was the target of or witnessed another's rage.

32. Assign the offender to write out a description of physical or emotional abuse that he/she has experienced as a child; process this material in session, identifying the feelings that are generated.

33. Ask the offender to write a letter that expresses his/her feelings to the parent figure responsible for uncontrollable anger in his/her own childhood; process this letter in session.

34. Explore the offender's feelings about whether he/she has the right to assertively ask for others to change their behavior.

35. Explore with the offender how it feels to display appropriate assertive behaviors within the family context.

36. Discuss with the offender how a lack of assertiveness promotes the danger of a reoffense.

37. Help the offender to understand how repressing anger

20. Make a list of specific strategies of how to deal with anger, rage, and frustration, and incorporate these strategies into a relapse prevention plan. (38)

can lead to physical or verbal aggression or sexual offending.

38. Assist the offender in creating a list of anger management strategies (e.g., assertiveness, time-out, relaxation, journaling feelings) that will be a part of a relapse prevention plan.

__. _____
   _____
__. _____
   _____
__. _____
   _____

__. _____
   _____
__. _____
   _____
__. _____
   _____

DIAGNOSTIC SUGGESTIONS:

CD-9-CM	ICD-10-CM	DSM-5 Disorder, Condition, or Problem
312.34	F63.81	Intermittent Explosive Disorder
296.xx	F31.xx	Bipolar I Disorder
296.89	F31.81	Bipolar II Disorder
312.8	F91.x	Conduct Disorder
310.1	F07.0	Personality Change Due to Another Medical Condition
309.81	F43.10	Posttraumatic Stress Disorder
301.83	F60.3	Borderline Personality Disorder
301.7	F60.2	Antisocial Personality Disorder
301.0	F60.0	Paranoid Personality Disorder
301.81	F60.81	Narcissistic Personality Disorder
301.9	F60.9	Unspecified Personality Disorder
_____	_____	_____
_____	_____	_____

CLERIC OFFENDER

BEHAVIORAL DEFINITIONS

1. Use of the role as a cleric to manipulate victims of sexual abuse.
2. Use of religious beliefs to justify the sexual abuse/assault or to minimize the consequences on the victim.
3. Use of religious beliefs to deny the need for sex offender–specific treatment.
4. Is a pastor in a Protestant church.
5. Is a priest in a Catholic church.
6. Is a rabbi in a Jewish synagogue.
7. Is a leader of a fundamentalist religious sect.

__. _____
   _____
   _____
__. _____
   _____
   _____
__. _____
   _____

LONG-TERM GOALS

1. Acknowledge that the position of spiritual authority was used to manipulate victims.
2. Incorporate religious tenets into relapse prevention plan without using these beliefs to fortify cognitive distortions.
3. Accept and participate in sex offender–specific treatment, and incorporate relapse prevention into life.

4. Achieve a quality of life that is sex offense–free on a continuing basis, while practicing own faith.

—. _____
  _____
—. _____
  _____
—. _____
  _____

SHORT-TERM OBJECTIVES

1. Describe the history and nature of the sexual offenses committed. (1, 2)

2. Express feelings of shame, hurt, and anger that are associated with having the label of "sex offender." (3)

3. Cooperate with and complete all psychosexual, neurological, and neuropsychological assessment procedures as requested. (4, 5)

THERAPEUTIC INTERVENTIONS

1. Explore the offender's history and nature of sexual abuse, confronting denial and minimization.

2. Assign the offender the task of listing his/her victims, the nature of the offense, and the time and place of occurrence.

3. Explore the offender's feelings about being treated as a sex offender, rather than being referred to as a pastor, father, rabbi, or bishop, and the loss of this specialness of being a cleric.

4. Refer the offender for a thorough psychosexual evaluation to include an evaluation for affective disorders and character pathology.

5. Refer the offender for a neurological/neuropsychological evaluation for brain damage related to head injury, alcoholism, seizure disorder, or some other medical condition.

4. Verbalize an understanding of how religious beliefs can function as part of a system of cognitive distortions. (6)

5. Verbalize an accurate understanding of human sexuality. (7, 8)

6. Verbalize an accurate understanding of childhood sexual development. (9)

6. Explore the offender's use of religious beliefs to support denial and minimization [e.g., that his/her sexual crime was the devil's work or due to the Yetser HaRah (evil inclination), and/or that he/she has been healed and has no need for treatment]; help him/her to take responsibility for his/her sexually abusive behavior.

7. Explore the offender's factual knowledge, feelings, and misperceptions about sexuality (e.g., masturbation, homosexuality, intercourse); provide him/her with accurate information and/or refer him/her to reliable reading material (e.g., Planned Parenthood literature). Consult with probation/parole officer regarding approval for sexual content.

8. Empathize with the offender about how difficult it may be to have an open, honest discussion about sexuality and his/her crime.

9. Explore the offender's distortions about childhood sexual development; correct his/her misperceptions, and discuss appropriate boundaries with children.

7. Describe how sexual attitudes were shaped through family-of-origin experiences. (10, 11)

8. Identify and reduce the frequency of deviant fantasies. (12)

9. Verbalize an understanding that the admission, repentance, or confession of the offense is insufficient for the prevention of relapse. (13, 14, 15)

10. Explore the offender's early development for origins of personal sexual attitudes, victimization, and/or parental attitudes toward sexuality that promoted shame or secrecy.

11. Assist the offender in completing a family genogram addressing repressive edicts in his/her family of origin regarding sexuality and how repression in general may have been encouraged. Address issues regarding sex being viewed as evil and carnal, and natural curiosity being discouraged or punished.

12. Assign the offender to complete the deviant arousal chapter in *Walk the Walk* (Horton), and then review insights that he/she has gained. (See the Deviant Arousal chapter in the Offender Issues part of this Planner.)

13. Teach the offender that repentance means a change in behavior, doing whatever is necessary in order not to repeat the sexual offense.

14. Assign the offender to read Chapter 3 in *Walk the Walk* (Horton) and complete the assignments.

15. Use the offender's own religious tenets (e.g., Bible quotes, Torah) to support the treatment process and to help encourage his/her participation; address his/her concept of evil (e.g., devil, Yetser HaRah,

10. Verbalize an increased understanding of how personal conflicts and a history of emotional trauma may have had an influence in the choice of occupation as a cleric. (16)

11. Identify and replace cognitive distortions used to maintain functioning as a cleric while committing sexually abusive/assaultive crimes. (17, 18)

demons), and incorporate taking responsibility for his/her offense.

16. Explore with the offender how a desire to resolve his/her personal issues stemming from a dysfunctional childhood perhaps motivated his/her choice of occupation and that his/her emotional instability may have predisposed him/her to act out in an exploitive/abusive manner.

17. Assist the offender in identifying and writing down the cognitive distortions he/she used to justify sexual abuse (e.g., I am showing the victim God's love; I am helping the victim feel pleasure; sex between adults and children is common, helps the child feel loved, and has an ancient history; I am merely teaching sexual freedom).

18. Replace the distorted cognitive messages that justify sexual abuse with realistic messages (e.g., sexual abuse is not a revelation of God's love but a self-centered exploitation; sex abuse is not pleasurable for the victim, but it is harmful; children are not to be exploited sexually, but protected and nurtured; sexual freedom is addressed through therapy, reading, and encouragement with consenting adults, not self-exploitation and abuse of power).

12. Verbally recognize dysfunctional motivations influencing the decision to become a cleric. (19)

19. Review with the offender his/her motivations involved in the decision to become a cleric, and confront his/her cognitive distortions associated with using his/her vocation, or calling, to control deviant sexual desires (e.g., a desire to be healed of deviant sexual thoughts or taking a vow of celibacy in order to combat fears of acting on deviant sexual thoughts).

13. List the ways in which the victim was manipulated into cooperating with and keeping silent about the sexual abuse. (20)

20. Assist the offender in listing the manipulations that he/she used on the sexual abuse victim (e.g., showing the victim God's love, targeting vulnerable individuals, using the position of power, taking advantage of the victim's trust); address the outer symbols of power and authority and how these were used to intimidate the victim (e.g., the cross hanging on a chain around the neck of a minister during the sexual assault, the gold and silver robes the priest wore while fondling a young boy in the confessional).

14. Acknowledge how the congregation and the victim have been negatively affected by the consequences of the sexual offense. (21, 22)

21. Review the consequences to the victim of the sexual abuse/assault and encourage the offender's empathy.

22. Explore the consequences to the congregation and how they are affected by their leader's sexually abusive behaviors (e.g., the congregation's feelings of

15. Bishop enforces the requirement for the priest to cooperate with sex offender–specific treatment. (23)

16. Priest relates cognitive distortions that justify sex abuse based on celibacy beliefs. (24)

17. Openly acknowledge and discuss any homosexual feelings. (25, 26, 27)

betrayal, denial, spiritual crisis, disillusionment); address the spiritual trauma to all who trusted the offender.

23. Consult with bishop and use the "vow of obedience" in order to counter the resistance of the priest-offender to submit to a psychosexual evaluation or attend sex offender–specific treatment.

24. Explore the offender's perception and belief regarding celibacy-related issues (e.g., celibacy is more pleasing to God, compared with being married; celibacy is viewed as a way to escape deviant fantasies) and his/her use of denial (e.g., the vow of celibacy forbids marriage to a woman but does not prohibit sexual activity nor sexual abuse/assault). Relate these issues to the offender's cognitive distortions, which he/she used to justify sexual assault.

25. Assist the offender in acknowledging his/her heterosexual/homosexual arousal, exploring legally and morally acceptable means of expression.

26. Explore whether the offender perceived an encouragement by superiors toward homosexual relationships in the priesthood.

18. Identify negative cognitive messages that trigger shame and anxiety related to sexuality because of religious beliefs and training. (28)

19. Acknowledge feelings of loneliness related to the clergy role, and identify potential sources of social and emotional support. (29)

20. Outline the boundaries on sexual practice that are dictated by religious beliefs. (30)

21. Verbalize an understanding of the impact of sexual offense on the lives of own friends and family. (31)

22. Verbalize an accurate understanding of how difficult it was for the victim to report the sexual abuse/assault. (32, 33)

27. Refer the priest-offender to a chapter of Courage (see www.couragerc.net) to gain support in living in accordance to the Catholic Church's teaching regarding homosexuality, or Dignity (see www.dignityusa.org) for an alternative approach.

28. Explore the role of religious training that promoted feelings of guilt and shame surrounding normal sexual behavior and desires.

29. Assist the offender in developing an insight into his/her feelings of isolation and loneliness while he/she was a cleric (along with the demands on a cleric's family) and how difficulty in coping with these feelings may have contributed to offense. Help the offender to develop an appropriate support system within his/her denomination to cope with stresses of life.

30. Explore with the offender the guidelines of his/her specific religion regarding sexuality and its boundaries.

31. Explore with the offender how his/her betrayal of trust affects the community within which he/she lives (e.g., his/her friends and family members).

32. Encourage the offender to express empathy for the victim and how difficult it may have been for the victim to reveal the sexual abuse. (Use a role-reversal technique to promote the offender's empathy for the victim's feelings.)

23. Verbalize a rejection of religious beliefs that promote illegal and demeaning behavior toward others. (34)

24. Cooperate with the inclusion of supervisory clergy in treatment. (35)

25. Take steps to make amends to members of the church/ synagogue. (36)

26. Identify alternative ways to feel empowered that are moral, ethical, and respectful of others. (37)

33. Lead the offender to acknowledge how his/her place of authority in the congregation may have prevented the victim from reporting the offense.

34. Explore the offender's religious beliefs that are illegal, demeaning, or inappropriate, and help him/her to understand the legal consequences of continuing such beliefs (e.g., child brides, child molestation, polygamy, severe corporal punishment for children).

35. Facilitate the participation of the family and religious hierarchy (e.g., bishop, supervising minister or rabbi) in treatment sessions for a coordination of care.

36. Integrate the members of the parish/congregation/synagogue into the offender's relapse prevention plan (e.g., restitution, restorative justice, letter of apology to the congregation); help the offender acknowledge spiritual trauma perpetrated upon the congregation.

37. Explore the issues of power and control with the offender, probing his/her family history for inconsistencies of authority figures and discipline methods; address alternative and healthier ways to cope with the need for control.

27. Supervisory personnel terminate denial and acknowledge the illegal behavior of the cleric. (38)

28. Participate in an accountability group with honest, open communication as part of the relapse prevention plan. (39)

29. Verbalize feelings about the losses resulting from the sexual offense behavior. (40, 41)

38. Communicate with the cleric-offender's religious superiors to address the denial within the hierarchical system that may have allowed the sexual abuse/assault to continue; assist them in determining an appropriate employment placement and treatment for the offender.

39. Assign the offender to an accountability group as part of the relapse prevention plan (see Chapter 4 in *Walk the Walk* by Horton); identify at least five individuals who will be supervisory persons.

40. Process grief and loss feelings with the offender regarding the possibility of reassignment, laicization, suspension, being disfellowshipped or defrocked.

41. Encourage the offender to rely upon his/her faith-based activities (e.g., prayer, meditation worship) and appropriate adult fellowship as sources of support in coping with losses due to his/her offense.

__. _____
    _____
__. _____
    _____
__. _____
    _____

__. _____
    _____
__. _____
    _____
__. _____
    _____

DIAGNOSTIC SUGGESTIONS:

ICD-9-CM	_ICD-10-CM_	_DSM-5_ Disorder, Condition, or Problem
300.4	F34.1	Persistent Depressive Disorder
296.xx	F32.x	Major Depressive Disorder, Single Episode
296.xx	F33.x	Major Depressive Disorder, Recurrent Episode
300.02	F41.1	Generalized Anxiety Disorder
312.34	F63.81	Intermittent Explosive Disorder
303.90	F10.20	Alcohol Use Disorder, Moderate or Severe
305.00	F10.10	Alcohol Use Disorder, Mild
301.9	F60.9	Unspecified Personality Disorder
301.7	F60.2	Antisocial Personality Disorder
301.50	F60.4	Histrionic Personality Disorder
301.81	F60.81	Narcissistic Personality Disorder
_____	_____	_____
_____	_____	_____

COGNITIVE DISTORTIONS

BEHAVIORAL DEFINITIONS

1. Sexual offending behaviors are supported by distorted cognitive assumptions, attitudes, and thinking patterns.
2. Avoids taking responsibility for own sexually abusive/assaultive behaviors through the use of justification, minimization, or denial.
3. Consistent pattern of blaming the victim for the sexual offense as a primary coping mechanism to avoid shame and guilt.
4. Verbalizes excuses for sexually abusive behaviors.
5. Minimizes sexually abusive behaviors.
6. Displays a lack of understanding and empathy for the depth of the pain of the victim and family members.

—. _____
   _____
   _____
—. _____
   _____
   _____
—. _____
   _____
   _____

LONG-TERM GOALS

1. Identify and remediate deviant cognitive patterns that support sexual abuse.
2. Attribute responsibility to self rather than blame others for the choice to offend.
3. Identify ways to disrupt deviant thinking, and instill new and more appropriate ways of thinking.

4. Acknowledge the harmful effect that the sexual abuse has had on the victim, the family, and society.

—. _____
   _____

—. _____
   _____

—. _____
   _____

SHORT-TERM OBJECTIVES

1. Complete assessment instruments designed to identify thinking errors. (1)

2. Report an awareness of uncomfortable feelings regarding discussing the nature of own cognitive distortions and exposing faults to others. (2, 3)

3. Identify and describe the historical patterns of resolving conflicts and problems used by family members during the early years of development. (4, 5, 6)

THERAPEUTIC INTERVENTIONS

1. Assess the offender's cognitive distortions by using a structured psychologcal instrument (e.g., Hanson Sex Attitudes Questionnaire, Abel-Becker Cognition Scale, and/or Bumby Molest and Rape Scales).

2. Express empathy and warmth toward the offender, avoiding a confrontational style in order to minimize his/her manipulative responding, resistance, or decrease in self-esteem.

3. Explore the offender's feelings regarding disclosing his/her thoughts about others that support sexual abuse/assault.

4. Assist the offender in developing a family genogram to increase awareness of his/her family patterns of blaming others and attributing guilt and shame.

4. List defenses that are commonly used to cope with internal conflicts. (7)

5. Identify and replace distorted cognitive messages that support sexually abusive/assaultive behavior. (8, 9, 10)

5. Explore with the offender how members of his/her family of origin dealt with conflict through the use of violence or abandonment.

6. Explore early problem-solving patterns that were used by family members during the offender's childhood.

7. Assist in developing a list of defenses that the offender uses to deal with any internal conflict (e.g., denial, rationalization, projection, minimization).

8. Assist the offender in identifying the cognitive distortions that he/she uses regarding sexual assault (e.g., complete denial of committing any of the abusive acts, denial of the harm of the abusive acts, minimizing the frequency or degree of the abuse, blaming the abusive acts on the victim). (See *Treating Child Sex Offenders and Victims* by Salter.)

9. Have the offender verbally list and refute common cognitive distortions of sex offenders (e.g., "we loved each other"; "she deserved to be raped because she was dressed like a prostitute"; "he's too young to remember so it won't bother him") with the help of the therapist and/or group members.

6. List the benefits of replacing cognitive distortions with accurate thinking. (11, 12)

7. Identify false assumptions held about the roles and feelings of males and females. (13, 14)

10. Challenge the offender's distorted cognitions that support his/her sexually offensive behavior, and replace each with a realistic, accurate thought.

11. Ask the offender to speculate what effect it would have on his/her self-esteem if he/she ceased to use offense-related cognitive distortions.

12. Ask the offender to list the personal benefits for letting go of his/her cognitive distortions (e.g., an increase in self-respect, lower likelihood of going to jail, decreased anxiety).

13. Explore whether the offender believes common fallacies about males that can nurture sexual abuse (e.g., men can't control themselves when it comes to sex; men don't have feelings like women do; a man is the owner of his family), and assign the offender to read *Men Who Rape* (Groth).

14. Explore whether the offender believes common, mistaken beliefs/assumptions about females (e.g., some women want to be raped; a woman should be submissive to a man; women may say no to sex but really mean yes).

8. Define consent regarding sexual activity and the factors that influence consent. (15, 16)

15. Help the offender to explore the definition of *consent* for a sexual encounter and who is and is not legally able to give consent; assign him/her to discuss this issue with significant others, bringing information back to the therapy session or group.

16. Teach the offender how to differentiate types of consent (e.g., a person consenting to going out on a date does not indicate that the individual is also consenting to sex) and the factors that influence consent (e.g., age, intimidation, size and strength, alcohol or drug use, position of authority).

9. Acknowledge that consent for sex can be retracted. (17)

17. Help the offender to explore feelings and an appropriate response to being in the middle of a sexual encounter when the partner decides to stop the physical contact, retracting apparent or implied consent.

10. Acknowledge own victimization history and its impact on the decision to victimize others. (18, 19, 20)

18. Explore the offender's own sexual abuse history. (See the chapters in the Victim Issues part of this Planner.)

19. Assist the offender in examining his/her own experiences as a victim and the feelings that he/she had during and after being abused.

20. Help the offender to see that, although he/she may have been sexually victimized, this does not give him/her the right or the excuse to sexually assault others; instead, his/her own victimization must sensitize him/her to the pain of being a target of abuse.

11. Verbalize ambivalent feelings about being an underage adolescent male victim who was sexually abused by an older adult woman. (21)

21. Help the male offender to express mixed feelings that he may have about being molested by an older girl/ woman; rectify the distorted viewpoint that the molestation was a prized sexual initiation.

12. Identify ways in which religious beliefs can become the basis for cognitive distortions and serve as a means of avoiding the difficult feelings of guilt and shame. (22, 23)

22. Teach the offender about the defense mechanism of religiosity, then ask him/her to list the religious reasons that he/she is using to avoid pursuing treatment (e.g., "God has healed me"; "God has forgiven me, and I need to forget about it").

23. If the offender is a minister, priest, rabbi, or other religious clergy, discuss how this position of power and cognitive distortions connected to their faith teachings were used in the sexual assault. (See the Cleric Offenders chapter in the Offender Issues part of this Planner.)

13. Verbalize how religion may be used positively to support recovery. (24, 25)

24. Assign the offender to consult with a minister, rabbi, or priest to discuss spiritual aspects of his/her recovery, and discuss this with the therapist and/or group.

14. Journal cognitive distortions that function to reduce personal responsibility for sexually abusive behavior and avoid guilt and shame. (26)

15. Practice identifying cognitive distortions by homework assignments. (27, 28)

16. List the reasons why it is difficult to admit to being solely responsible for the sexual abuse. (29)

17. Verbalize prosocial thoughts regarding the inappropriateness of sexual contact between adults and children. (30, 31)

25. Assign the offender to locate and write Bible verses (e.g., Matthew 18:6; I Corinthians 6:9; Galatians 5:19) or other sacred or spiritual writings that condemn sexual victimization.

26. Assign the offender to journal his/her incidents of cognitive distortions, and guide him/her in the use of self-management techniques to improve or reverse distorted thinking.

27. Assign the offender to watch the movie *Clean and Sober* starring Michael Keaton; critique the behavior of the character played by Keaton and identify and describe his cognitive distortions.

28. Assign the offender to read *The True Story of the 3 Little Pigs! By A. Wolf* (Scieszka and Smith) and identify cognitive distortions used.

29. Have the offender list the reasons why it is difficult to admit the sexual assault (e.g., shame and guilt, angry reactions from family, fear of being prosecuted).

30. Explore the offender's view regarding sexual contact between children and adults; confront and correct cognitive distortions.

31. Assist the offender in listing reasons why sexual contact between an adult and a child is harmful (e.g., children are unable to consent; children are taught that affection is paired with sexuality; children are emotionally immature).

18. List the qualities and advantages of being involved in emotionally healthy, equitable, age-appropriate social and romantic relationships. (32, 33)

19. Develop an aftercare plan of new life goals, which includes moral and ethical standards. (34, 35)

32. Help the offender to incorporate into his/her self-concept the idea of looking for a partner who is age-appropriate and consenting; teach the advantages (e.g., potential for genuine intimacy, equality, and empathic support) of being involved in intimate interactions that do not involve manipulation, force, deception, abuse of authority or power, or threats.

33. Have the offender list the qualities of healthy intimate relationships (e.g., honesty, effective communication, mutual emotional support), and process this information with the therapy group or the individual therapist.

34. Assist the offender in developing a prosocial life purpose, living a life that is driven by moral and ethical values, not dependent on reduction of negative affect by distorted thinking.

35. Rather than emphasizing the negative aspects that the offender has to eliminate, help him/her to develop a life plan that indicates what he/she should do positively to live a moral, ethical life.

__. _____

__. _____

__. _____

__. _____

__. _____

__. _____

DIAGNOSTIC SUGGESTIONS:

ICD-9-CM	*ICD-10-CM*	*DSM-5* Disorder, Condition, or Problem
300.4	F34.1	Persistent Depressive Disorder
296.xx Episode	F32.x	Major Depressive Disorder, Single
296.xx Episode	F33.x	Major Depressive Disorder, Recurrent
305.00	F10.10	Alcohol Use Disorder, Mild
303.90 Severe	F10.20	Alcohol Use Disorder, Moderate or
312.34	F63.81	Intermittent Explosive Disorder
302.4	F65.2	Exhibitionistic Disorder
302.81	F65.0	Fetishistic Disorder
302.89	F65.81	Frotteuristic Disorder
302.2	F65.4	Pedophilic Disorder
302.83	F65.51	Sexual Masochism Disorder
302.84	F65.52	Sexual Sadism Disorder
302.82	F65.3	Voyeuristic Disorder
302.89	F65.9	Unspecified Paraphilic Disorder
301.9	F60.9	Unspecified Personality Disorder
301.7	F60.2	Antisocial Personality Disorder
301.81	F60.81	Narcissistic Personality Disorder
_____	_____	_____
_____	_____	_____

DENIAL

BEHAVIORAL DEFINITIONS

1. Consistently denies being the perpetrator of the sexual abuse or assault.
2. Denies experiencing deviant sexual fantasies and arousal.
3. Denies the harmful effects of the sexual abuse/assault on the victim, family, and society.
4. Makes a partial admission of the criminal sexual assault, using excuses to moderate culpability.
5. Distorts the facts of the crime to minimize responsibility and harm.

—. _____
   _____

—. _____
   _____

—. _____
   _____

LONG-TERM GOALS

1. Demonstrate an increased acceptance of responsibility for the criminal sexual conduct.
2. Reduce the depth of denial through participation in victim empathy training.
3. Reduce denial of deviant sexual arousal.

4. Increase veracity of the description of the sexual offense, concurring with the account given by the victim.

___. _____

_____

___. _____

_____

___. _____

_____

SHORT-TERM OBJECTIVES

THERAPEUTIC INTERVENTIONS

1. Acknowledge that it is difficult to admit being responsible for criminal sexual activity. (1)

1. Use warmth and empathy to encourage the offender to disclose his/her responsibility for the sexual assault; show understanding regarding how difficult it is to admit to himself/herself and others that he/she has committed a heinous crime.

2. Verbalize an understanding of denial as a common defense mechanism. (2)

2. Normalize denial as common in the early stages of treatment, and clarify the negative impact of denial on the later stages of treatment.

3. Verbalize an understanding that denial allows for avoidance of difficult feelings. (3, 4)

3. Assist the offender in understanding how postoffense denial functions to avoid the feelings of guilt and shame. (See the Guilt/Shame chapter in the Offender Issues part of this Planner.)

4. Encourage the offender to discriminate between his/her criminal behavior and his/her worth as a person; model respect for the offender

4. Acknowledge reasons for denial and problem-solve how to cope with negative affect in a more positive manner. (5, 6, 7)

5. Identify the consequences that are feared and, therefore, support denial. (8)

while discussing the serious nature of the offense.

5. Discuss with the offender in a hypothetical manner why he/she might be in denial. Direct other group members to talk about how their own denial early in treatment allowed for avoidance of guilt and shame feelings.

6. Ask the offender to speculate on what his/her feelings about himself/herself would be if the offense were true and he/she admitted it (e.g., shame, humiliation, sadness), and ways to deal with these painful emotions other than denial.

7. Teach the offender healthier, honest, and constructive ways to cope with guilt and shame (e.g., exploring own feelings and labeling them honestly, journaling feelings, sharing feelings in therapy or self-help group, sharing feelings with a trusted friend or family member, confessing feelings to a clergy member or directly to God). (See the Guilt/Shame chapter in the Offender Issues part of this Planner.)

8. Probe for fears that continue to support the offender's denial (e.g., fear of incarceration, family loss, being shunned by society).

6. Cooperate with submitting to a polygraph examination. (9)

7. Verify the veracity of own trial transcripts that confirm guilt. (10)

8. Acknowledge the use of pornography and other sexually deviant practices. (11)

9. Identify types of denial and cognitive distortions that promote sexually abusive behaviors. (12, 13)

9. Request from the probation/-parole officer that a polygraph examination be administered to the offender in order to assist the offender in overcoming his/her denial and minimization.

10. Request a transcript of the trial proceedings (if available) during which the offender admitted guilt; confront him/her with this information in individual or group therapy.

11. Consult with the offender's probation/parole officer whether the examination of the offender's place of living yielded evidence of pornography, sexually related items, pictures of children, or Internet sex material; confront the offender's denial of sexual fantasies or behaviors that increase the risk of relapse. Use information from phallometric testing, polygraphy, viewing time measures, and psychosexual evaluation.

12. Explore the different types of denial (e.g., admitting the act, but justifying the behavior; minimizing the crime; denying the need for treatment), evaluating the offender's words or behaviors for evidence of denial. (See *Treating Child Sex Offenders and Victims* by Salter.)

10. List behavioral and fantasy practices that nurture sexually abusive behavior. (14)

11. Verbalize an increased awareness of the harmful impact that denial has on the victim. (15)

12. Participate in drama therapy to increase expression of affect regarding own victimization and feelings of empathy toward the victim. (16, 17)

13. Assist the offender in listing the cognitive distortions that are commonly used to blame the victim for the offense. (See the Cognitive Distortions chapter in the Offender Issues part of this Planner.)

14. Assist the offender in compiling a list of 10 behavioral or fantasy practices that increase the likelihood of committing a sexual offense (e.g., reading sadomasochistic pornography, surfing the Internet for vulnerable children, stalking children or other targets of abuse, attending adult theaters); process the list material.

15. Assist the offender in making a list of the ways that his/her denial can hurt the victim (e.g., victim may continue to blame self for the abuse; victim will not be able to confront the offender during clarification or restorative justice session; some of the victim's family members may continue to believe the victim was fabricating the offense).

16. Assist the offender in reenactment aspects (drama therapy) of his/her sexual crimes and his/her own victimization to increase the connection to his/her affect and to decrease his/her denial; ask the offender to reverse roles, playing his/her victim and then his/her own perpetrator, sharing feelings during the process.

13. Describe the disadvantages of continuing to maintain denial in the treatment process. (18)

14. Identify the relationships that are supportive and those that are nonsupportive of treatment and of denial. (19, 20)

15. Verbalize remorse about having sexually assaulted the victim. (21, 22)

17. Remain aware of how the offender may attempt to manipulate the therapist and/or group members, and confront him/her when this happens.

18. Review with the offender the negative impact that denial has on treatment (e.g., impedes progress, increases reoffense risk, increases anxiety).

19. Direct the offender to withdraw from relationships that support his/her denial (e.g., drinking buddies or individuals who refuse to accept the reality of his/her sexual offense); assist him/her in identifying and listing those negative relationships.

20. Assign the offender to give verbal permission to those in his/her support system to confront his/her denial, question his/her behavior, and communicate their concerns to the therapist and/or the probation/parole officer.

21. Contact the offender's probation/parole officer, and request a copy of the victim impact statement or other legal paperwork containing statements describing the sexual assault.

22. Review the victim impact statement with the offender, exploring his/her emotional reaction to hearing about the trauma of the sexual assault from the victim's perspective.

16. List the long-term harmful effects of sexual assault on the victim, and express an accurate understanding of the victim's pain. (23)

17. Write an accurate and detailed account of the sexual assault, taking full responsibility for the crime. (24)

18. Verbalize feelings of empathy for the victim by cooperating with expressive therapy procedures. (25)

19. Role-play the offense from the victim's perspective including thoughts, feelings, and physical descriptors. (26, 27)

23. Assign the offender to research and list the long-term harmful effects of sexual trauma on victims (e.g., emotional, physical, social) and to present this list to the therapist or the therapy group.

24. Assign the offender to write a victim clarification statement; assist him/her in revising the statement to increase the clarity of his/her statements of responsibility for the offenses and its harmful impact on the victim. (See *Just Before Dawn* by Hindman.)

25. Use art therapy to increase the offender's contact with his/her affect and to decrease denial (e.g., draw a picture of how he/she thinks the victim may have felt, a picture of his/her own inner child, or a picture of himself/herself as a victim).

26. During a drama therapy session, assign the offender to play the role of the victim asking the offender to stop the abuse; process the feelings that are generated.

27. Assign the offender to role-play the viewpoint of his/her victim, and have the group critique the role play and identify cognitive distortions used by him/her regarding the offense.

20. Verbalize statements that show respect and honor for the victim. (28)

21. Cooperate with a referral to a pretreatment sex offender's group that is focused on denial issues. (29, 30, 31)

28. To encourage an empathic response to the victim, ask the offender to write a poem or draw a picture to honor the victim.

29. Assign the offender to a *pretreatment group* with other denying offenders, where admitting the offense is a requirement to graduate to a regular offender's group. Treat by education and addressing other dysfunctional areas in the offender's life.

30. Place the offender in a pretreatment group where time accumulated does not count toward a favorable report to the state parole board or toward satisfying treatment requirements.

31. Assign the offender to a structured, time-limited pretreatment group that will focus on the denial issue. [See "Treating Sex Offenders Who Deny Their Guilt: A Pilot Study" by Schlank and Shaw in *Sexual Abuse: A Journal of Research and Treatment,* or "Working with Denial in Sexual Abusers: Some Clinical Suggestions" by Bays in *Handbook for Sexual Abuser Assessment and Treatment* (Carich and Mussack, eds.).]

22. Verbalize insights learned from talking and listening to offenders who have successfully overcome their own denial. (32)

23. Accept referral to a *categorical denial* sex offender's group, and comply with participation and assignment requirements. (33, 34, 35)

32. Refer the offender to an ongoing structured sex offenders' group, composed of all admitting offenders where, in part of each session, other members will address the offender's cognitive distortions that support denial. Set a time limit for breaking denial, working with the probation/parole officer and the court regarding the consequences of continued denial.

33. Refer the offender who is in categorical denial to a structured sex offender treatment group with other deniers in which there is no requirement to admit the offense, but the offenders are educated about offense cycles, coping strategies, and victim impact. (See "Treatment of Sexual Offenders Who Are in Categorical Denial: A Pilot Project" by Marshall, Thornton, Marshall, Fernandez, and Mann in *Sexual Abuse: A Journal of Research and Treatment*.)

34. Require the denying offender to attend one extra group per week, indicating that when denial is decreased, treatment requirement frequency would also decrease.

35. Change the goals of treatment to improving overall functioning and addressing consequences of future errors in judgment regarding sexual behavior that could lead to another conviction.

24. Cooperate with reassessment procedures to determine the necessity for alternative treatment plans. (36)

36. Administer the Psychopathy Checklist—Revised (PCL-R) to evaluate the offender for psychopathy and to assess risk; if the offender receives a high PCL-R score, this may be a contraindication for successful sex offender treatment and would require consultation with the offender's probation/parole officer regarding risk for relapse and placement issues.

__. _____

__. _____

__. _____

__. _____

__. _____

__. _____

DIAGNOSTIC SUGGESTIONS:

ICD-9-CM	ICD-10-CM	DSM-5 Disorder, Condition, or Problem
300.4	F34.1	Persistent Depressive Disorder
296.xx	F32.x	Major Depressive Disorder, Single Episode
296.xx	F33.x	Major Depressive Disorder, Recurrent Episode
305.00	F10.10	Alcohol Use Disorder, Mild
303.90	F10.20	Alcohol Use Disorder, Moderate or Severe
312.34	F63.81	Intermittent Explosive Disorder
302.4	F65.2	Exhibitionistic Disorder
302.81	F65.0	Fetishistic Disorder

302.89	F65.81	Frotteuristic Disorder
302.2	F65.4	Pedophilic Disorder
302.83	F65.51	Sexual Masochism Disorder
302.84	F65.52	Sexual Sadism Disorder
302.82	F65.3	Voyeuristic Disorder
302.89	F65.9	Unspecified Paraphilic Disorder
301.9	F60.9	Unspecified Personality Disorder
301.7	F60.2	Antisocial Personality Disorder
301.81	F60.81	Narcissistic Personality Disorder
_____	_____	_____
_____	_____	_____

DEVIANT SEXUAL AROUSAL

BEHAVIORAL DEFINITIONS

1. Sexual arousal associated with the exposure of the genitals to an unsuspecting stranger (exhibitionism).
2. Sexual arousal associated with the use of nonliving objects (e.g., female undergarments, shoes, rubber clothing) (fetishism).
3. Sexual arousal associated with touching and rubbing against a nonconsenting person (frotteurism).
4. Sexual arousal associated with a desire for sexual activity with a prepubescent child (pedophilia).
5. Sexual arousal associated with the act of being humiliated, beaten, bound, or otherwise made to suffer (sexual masochism).
6. Sexual arousal associated with the psychological or physical suffering on the part of the victim (sexual sadism).
7. Sexual arousal associated with cross-gender dressing (transvestic fetishism).
8. Sexual arousal associated with the act of observing an unsuspecting person who is naked, in the process of disrobing, or engaged in sexual activity (voyeurism).
9. Sexual arousal to abusive, violent, or deviant themes is greater than arousal to appropriate sexual themes.
10. Sexual interest as measured by phallometric assessment or viewing time measures results in a disordered sexual arousal profile.
11. A tendency to engage in deviant sexual practices when under stress.
12. Sexual arousal associated with unconventional or bizarre objects, people, or activities.

__. _____
    _____
__. _____
    _____

—.　_____

_____

LONG-TERM GOALS

1. Reduce and control deviant fantasies and arousal.
2. Increase and sustain arousal to appropriate sexual themes.
3. Develop alternative coping strategies and learn more prosocial ways to deal with emotional needs rather than masturbating to or acting out deviant fantasies.
4. Decrease the covert rehearsal of deviant fantasies.

—.　_____

_____

—.　_____

_____

—.　_____

_____

SHORT-TERM OBJECTIVES	THERAPEUTIC INTERVENTIONS
1. Participate in a thorough assessment of the sexual arousal pattern (e.g., consenting to plethysmography, or measure of sexual interest; agreeing to consultation of collateral sources of information). (1)	1. Perform a thorough assessment of the offender's sexual arousal pattern. This should include gathering his/her own report, masturbatory history, arousal to violence, and collateral information (e.g., victim statement, and phallometric data or the Abel Assessment for sexual interest).
2. Disclose all sexual fantasies to the therapist. (2)	2. Encourage the offender to reveal sexual fantasies even though he/she may be feeling anxiety or shame; assess the frequency, strength, detail, and length of time given to the fantasies.

3. Keep a daily journal outlining sexual fantasies, thoughts, and feelings. (3, 4, 5)

4. Verbalize the connection between the avoidance of experiencing difficult emotions and engaging in the use of deviant sexual fantasies. (5, 6)

5. Verbalize to other group members the occurrence of sexual fantasies and discuss related feelings. (7)

6. Agree to participate in a behavior modification program focused on decreasing deviant sexual activity. (8, 9, 10, 11)

3. Assign the offender to keep a daily journal of his/her sexual fantasies, thoughts, or feelings.

4. Help the offender to understand how deviant fantasies are related to his/her offending behavior by exploring for examples of the thoughts leading to that behavior.

5. Assign the offender the task of listing situations or uncomfortable feelings that have triggered escapist deviant fantasies.

6. Explore how engaging in deviant sexual fantasies is frequently a way to avoid emotional discomfort or painful feelings.

7. Assign the task of describing to other members in a sex offender group how the avoidance of difficult feelings led to deviant sexual fantasies.

8. Urge voluntary participation in a behavior modification program designed to reduce deviant sexual activity.

9. Encourage the offender to adopt an attitude of collaboration with the therapist in choosing behavior modification techniques geared toward deviant arousal reduction.

7. Verbalize fears to therapist regarding behavior modification program and ask questions prior to consent. (11, 12)

8. Express an understanding of the olfactory aversion technique, and participate in a thorough medical evaluation and consultation with a primary care physician. (13)

9. Define consensual sex and what *normal and healthy* sexuality means. (14)

10. Cooperate with an implementation of the behavior modification treatment procedure. (15)

10. Discuss with the offender specific behavior modification choices (e.g., olfactory aversion, covert sensitization, assisted covert sensitization, masturbatory reconditioning, verbal satiation, or some combination of these techniques).

11. Explain behavior modification procedures and potential risks to the offender in detail (e.g., increased anxiety or depression), and have him/her sign an informed consent release.

12. Process the offender's fears about the behavior modification procedures.

13. If olfactory aversion therapy using ammonia is going to be implemented, recommend that the offender get a medical evaluation and the consent of his/her primary care physician before starting behavior modification regimen.

14. Assist the offender in outlining an appropriate sexual fantasy that includes a loving adult partner who voluntarily engages in the sexual act in a loving, cooperative manner.

15. Train the offender in the mechanics of the behavior modification program (e.g., olfactory aversion, covert sensitization, masturbatory reconditioning, verbal satiation) with the deviant fantasies as the target symptom.

11. Collaborate in a modification of the treatment plan by revealing any recurrence of deviant fantasies and openly discussing fantasies and precursors. (16)

12. Verbalize an acceptance that self-monitoring is a full-time job, and list situations and places that can easily lead to an increase in inappropriate sexual fantasies. (17, 18)

13. Identify areas in life of unmet needs (e.g., lack of close friends, fears of intimacy, struggles with spirituality). (19, 20)

16. Periodically reassess the success of the treatment plan and modify when needed.

17. Assist the offender in listing situations (e.g., being alone with a child, picking up a hitchhiker, spending time at the beach, living across the street from an elementary school) that stimulate deviant arousal.

18. Teach the offender to avoid places that may increase deviant arousal and to avoid masturbating to deviant fantasies so as not to reinforce the deviant arousal to an inappropriate stimulus.

19. Explore the offender's unmet needs (e.g., socialization, intimacy), and assist him/her in understanding how they contribute to the development of deviant sexual fantasies and deviant behavior as inappropriate substitutes.

20. Teach the offender how to get his/her normal needs (e.g., socialization, intimacy) met in more prosocial ways (e.g., seeking appropriate friendships, hobbies).

14. Participate in empathy training. (21)

15. Implement anger management techniques to assist in reducing frequency of deviant fantasy recurrence. (22)

16. Report a reduction in stress level due to using anxiety management techniques. (23)

17. Verbalize an understanding that deviant fantasies will recur, and outline specific coping mechanisms that will be implemented. (24, 25, 26)

21. Use role-playing, role-reversal, and empty-chair techniques to increase the offender's sensitivity to the needs, rights, and feelings of others.

22. Teach the offender anger management techniques (e.g., time-out, relaxation, assertiveness, recognizing triggers, practicing forgiveness, replacing distorted cognitive messages).

23. Teach the offender stress management techniques (e.g., deep muscle relaxation, positive guided imagery, physical exercise, replacing cognitive messages that mediate anxiety).

24. Stress to the offender that it is likely that deviant arousal themes or interests will return, and teach him/her coping strategies for when this does happen (e.g., contacting a therapist, reinstituting behavior modification techniques that have been effective in the past, asking for help in group therapy).

25. Process feelings with the offender when his/her deviant fantasies recur after an extended absence.

26. Encourage the offender to discuss feelings in group therapy regarding deviant fantasy recurrence.

18. Cooperate with a physician regarding a medication evaluation in order to assist with arousal control problems. (27)

19. Take medication as prescribed, communicating to the physician and the therapist effectiveness and side effects. (28)

27. If deviant fantasies are overpowering, send the offender for a medication evaluation to decrease sexual drive or reduce obsessive sexual thinking and to help him/her feel more in control and more amenable to psychotherapeutic interventions.

28. Discuss with the offender the effectiveness of the medication, and collaborate with his/her physician in outlining a treatment plan.

___. _____
   _____
___. _____
   _____
___. _____
   _____

___. _____
   _____
___. _____
   _____
___. _____
   _____

DIAGNOSTIC SUGGESTIONS:

ICD-9-CM	ICD-10-CM	DSM-5 Disorder, Condition, or Problem
302.4	F65.2	Exhibitionistic Disorder
302.81	F65.0	Fetishistic Disorder
302.89	F65.81	Frotteuristic Disorder
302.2	F65.4	Pedophilic Disorder

302.83	F65.51	Sexual Masochism Disorder
302.84	F65.52	Sexual Sadism Disorder
302.82	F65.3	Voyeuristic Disorder
302.89	F65.9	Unspecified Paraphilic Disorder
____	____	_____
____	____	_____

EMPATHY DEFICITS

BEHAVIORAL DEFINITIONS

1. Lack of awareness of the devastating short- and long-term emotional impact of sexual assault on the victim.
2. Consistent pattern of blaming the victim for the sexual assault.
3. Displays a lack of remorse for the sexual assault.
4. Difficulty in understanding what others feel and how intimate relationships are based on empathy and trust.
5. History of sexually inappropriate behaviors with little regard for boundaries.
6. Justifies having sex with children without regard to the negative effect on the child.

—. _____
   _____

—. _____
   _____

—. _____
   _____

LONG-TERM GOALS

1. Understand what empathy is and its importance in relationships.
2. Verbalize and internalize the unique damage that sexual abuse/assault causes the victim, family, and society.
3. Become skilled at identifying the impact of own behavior on the feelings of others, and modify behavior out of concern for others' feelings.
4. Develop the ability to respond appropriately and supportively to others in relationships.

5. Develop the basic social skills that are necessary to communicate appropriately and respectfully, especially with respect to difficult and powerful feelings.

___. _____
_____
_____

___. _____
_____
_____

___. _____
_____
_____

SHORT-TERM OBJECTIVES

1. Verbalize a definition of *empathy.* (1, 2)

2. List ways of demonstrating empathy. (2, 3)

THERAPEUTIC INTERVENTIONS

1. Teach the offender the meaning, consequences of, and need for empathy.

2. Help the offender to define concrete steps to express empathy (e.g., be able to recognize his/her own feelings, express his/her own feelings to others, identify feelings in others).

2. Help the offender to define concrete steps to express empathy (e.g., be able to recognize his/her own feelings, express his/her own feelings to others, identify feelings in others).

3. Help the offender to identify specific actions that indicate empathy (e.g., maintaining eye contact, asking questions, stating the feeling behind what has been said).

3. Describe the feelings experienced by fictional people. (4, 5)

4. Verbalize the differences between enabling, pity, and empathy. (6, 7)

5. Verbalize an understanding of how the lack of empathy from parental figures led to empathy deficits in self. (8, 9)

6. Acknowledge that empathy has been absent from own life. (10, 11)

4. Ask the offender to identify with a character in a movie and describe that character's feelings.

5. Assign the offender to imagine the feelings of a robbery victim, asking him/her to focus on the intensity of the feelings and describe them to others in the group. Have the group rate the offender's effectiveness in being empathic.

6. Teach the offender how self-pity prevents one from developing empathy.

7. Teach the offender the difference between empathy, enabling, and pity; ask him/her to give examples of how each can be demonstrated.

8. Explore the offender's history of not being shown empathy as a child and how that felt.

9. Assist the offender in writing a letter to his/her parent describing incidents when that parent did not have empathy and his/her feelings associated with those incidents; ask the offender to not send the letter, but read it aloud to the therapist or group.

10. Assist the offender in seeing the thought and behavior patterns that demonstrate a lack of empathy in his/her life. (See *Cognitive Behavioral Treatment of Sexual Offenders* by Marshall, Anderson, and Fernandez.)

7. Define *narcissism,* and contrast this to empathy. (6, 12, 13, 14)

11. Ask the offender to list his/her favorite jokes, and evaluate with him/her how his/her humor lacks empathy and may focus on the humiliation of others.

6. Teach the offender how self-pity prevents one from developing empathy.

12. Teach the offender a definition of narcissism or self-focus and how this attitude plays a significant part in his/her life.

13. Confront the offender when he/she makes narcissistic statements.

14. Assist the offender in making a list of how narcissism is different from empathy (e.g., constant self-focus versus the ability to focus on the needs of others; exploitation of others versus interactions with others, guided by conscience and morality; indifference to the feelings of others versus displaying empathic responses to others).

8. Write an accurate account of the sexual assault from the victim's perspective. (15, 16)

15. Assign the offender to go over the details of the sexual assault in the group and/or with the therapist.

16. Explore with the offender how the victim felt during the sexual assault, and have the offender present it to the group. (See *Cognitive Behavioral Treatment of Sexual Offenders* by Marshall, Anderson, and Fernandez.)

9. Verbalize an understanding of how the victim felt before, during, and after the sexual assault. (16, 17)

10. Identify the emotions that the victim feels now. (18, 19)

11. Verbalize the stages of loss and grief and how they apply to the recovery process of the victim. (20)

12. Terminate statements blaming the victim for the sexual assault. (10, 21, 22)

16. Explore with the offender how the victim felt during the sexual assault, and have the offender present it to the group. (See *Cognitive Behavioral Treatment of Sexual Offenders* by Marshall, Anderson, and Fernandez.)

17. Have the offender describe in detail, to another trusted adult, an empathic description of the victim's feelings, and have the listener give feedback.

18. Assist the offender in making a list of at least five feelings that the victim is likely to be experiencing now as the result of the crime (e.g., fear, depression, anger).

19. Use the empty-chair and role-reversal techniques to teach the offender sensitivity to the feelings of others, especially feelings resulting from his/her sexual abuse/assault.

20. Teach the offender the key concepts related to the stages of loss and grief, and assist him/her in applying these stages to the victim.

10. Assist the offender in seeing the thought and behavior patterns that demonstrate a lack of empathy in his/her life. (See *Cognitive Behavioral Treatment of Sexual Offenders* by Marshall, Anderson, and Fernandez.)

21. Confront the offender when he/she makes statements blaming the victim for the abuse.

22. Ask the offender to write a hypothetical letter to a family member who blames the victim for the abuse, convincing the family member that the abuse is the offender's fault.

13. Write the victim an apology letter (unsent). (23)

23. Assign the offender to write a letter (unsent) of apology to the victim (clarification); review the letter for genuine empathy and remorse. (See *Just Before Dawn* by Hindman.)

14. Express an understanding of the effect of the sexual assault on others, beyond just the victim. (24, 25, 26)

24. Have the offender describe how others who are connected to the crime feel (e.g., the parent of the victim, the police officer who made the arrest, the social worker who participated in the interview).

25. Elicit from the offender a verbal description of how the crime affected the victim's family immediately and how it will affect them in the future.

26. Assist the offender in understanding how others may not trust him/her because of his/her criminal sexual assault.

15. Make a commitment to develop empathy as a lifestyle in dealing with others. (27, 28, 29)

27. Assist the offender in outlining how he/she could practice empathy for others daily.

28. Help the offender to make a list of ways in which he/she can contribute to the community on a long-term basis without personal gain [e.g., making monetary contri-butions to charity, volunteering a service to a church (in keeping with his/her relapse prevention plan and with approval of the pro-bation/parole officer and con-sultation with the therapist), participating in a long-term aftercare program such as a sexual addiction 12-step group independent of the require-ments of probation).

29. Ask the offender to describe a time when someone showed disrespectful, nonempathic be-havior toward him/her and how that person may have im-proved the interaction.

16. Demonstrate empathy in ev-eryday interactions. (2, 30, 31, 32, 33)

2. Help the offender to define concrete steps to express em-pathy (e.g., be able to recog-nize his/her own feelings, express his/her own feelings to others, identify feelings in others).

30. Assign the offender the task of doing something kind for someone without their knowl-edge and to write about his/her own feelings and the feelings of the recipient.

31. Explore the offender's current relationships, and assist him/her in making empathic statements about people.

32. Assign the offender to make three empathic statements daily to family, friends, or group members and to record these statements in a journal.

33. Use role play, modeling, and behavior rehearsal to teach the offender how to express empathy.

17. Make three empathic statements daily. (19, 32, 33)

19. Use the empty-chair and role-reversal techniques to teach the offender sensitivity to the feelings of others, especially feelings resulting from his/her sexual abuse/assault.

32. Assign the offender to make three empathic statements daily to family, friends, or group members and to record the statements in a journal.

33. Use role play, modeling, and behavior rehearsal to teach the offender how to express empathy.

18. Write a justification for allowing the names and addresses of sex offenders to be available on the Internet and for requiring that sex offenders register with law enforcement authorities after a move. (34, 35)

34. Give the offender the assignment of justifying how the community in which he/she resides would benefit from his/her name being on an Internet list of sexual offenders.

35. Have the offender produce
    a written justification of why
    he/she must register
    in communities when he/
    she travels to other parts
    of the country.

19. Outline the consequences of
    the lack of empathy in rela-
    tionships. (8, 36)

8. Explore the offender's history
   of not being shown empathy
   as a child and how that felt.

36. Assist the offender in listing
    the consequences of a lack of
    empathy in relationships (e.g.,
    loss of trust, lack of intimacy,
    hurt feelings, defensive
    detachment).

20. Give a presentation to group
    or therapist about the immedi-
    ate and long-term
    effects of sexual abuse/
    assault. (16, 18, 25, 26, 37)

16. Explore with the offender how
    the victim felt during the sex-
    ual assault, and have the of-
    fender present it to the group.
    (See *Cognitive Behavioral
    Treatment of Sexual Offenders*
    by Marshall, Anderson, and
    Fernandez.)

18. Assist the offender in making
    a list of at least five feelings
    that the victim is likely to be
    experiencing now as the result
    of the crime (e.g., fear, depres-
    sion, anger).

25. Elicit from the offender a ver-
    bal description of how the
    crime affected the victim's
    family immediately and how it
    will affect them in the future.

26. Assist the offender in understanding how others may not trust him/her because of his/her criminal sexual assault.

37. Assign the offender to list the long- and short-term effects of his/her sexual abuse.

21. List ways to make restitution to those who have been hurt by own behavior. (23, 24, 38)

23. Assign the offender to write a letter (unsent) of apology to the victim (clarification); review the letter for genuine empathy and remorse. (See *Just Before Dawn* by Hindman.)

24. Have the offender describe how others who are connected to the crime feel (e.g., the parent of the victim, the police officer who made the arrest, the social worker who participated in the interview).

38. Assign the offender to list 10 individuals who have been harmed by him/her and how appropriate restitution might be made.

___. _____

_____

___. _____

_____

___. _____

_____

___. _____

_____

___. _____

_____

___. _____

_____

DIAGNOSTIC SUGGESTIONS:

ICD-9-CM	_ICD-10-CM_	_DSM-5_ Disorder, Condition, or Problem
312.8	F91.x	Conduct Disorder
302.9	F52.9	Unspecified Sexual Dysfunction
302.89	F65.9	Unspecified Paraphilic Disorder
302.2	F65.4	Pedophilic Disorder
301.7	F60.2	Antisocial Personality Disorder
301.81	F60.81	Narcissistic Personality Disorder

FEMALE OFFENDER

BEHAVIORAL DEFINITIONS

1. Committed sexual abuse of a prepubescent child.
2. Committed sexual abuse of an adolescent male or female.
3. Has a sexual attraction to children.
4. Yields to verbal or physical coercion by a male or female partner to abuse a related (e.g., son or daughter) or nonrelated child.
5. An active or passive partner of a male perpetrator who sexually abuses children.
6. Acquires a victim for a male coperpetrator of sexual assault.
7. Blames male coperpetrator for the sexual assault on others.
8. Difficulty in establishing and maintaining intimate adult relationships.
9. Emotionally immature, dependent, and has low self-esteem.

__. _____
   _____
__. _____
   _____
__. _____
   _____

LONG-TERM GOALS

1. Terminate inappropriate, illegal, sexually abusive behavior.
2. Acknowledge sexually abusive patterns and learn nonabusive ways to meet emotional needs.
3. Learn intimacy skills to be applied in adult relationships.
4. Regulate emotional arousal by means other than sexual behaviors and/or sexual abuse.

5. Increase self-esteem and assertively maintain healthy relationship boundaries.

—. _____

_____

—. _____

_____

—. _____

_____

SHORT-TERM OBJECTIVES

1. Describe the nature and history of the sexually
   abusive/assaultive behav-ior,
   and comply with the
   request for a psychosexual
   evaluation. (1, 2)

2. Describe childhood experiences of physical, sexual, and
   emotional abuse. (2, 3, 4, 5)

THERAPEUTIC INTERVENTIONS

1. Explore the offender's history
   and nature of sexual offenses,
   including review of pertinent
   court and mental health
   records.

2. Build the level of trust with
   the offender through empathic
   statements, eye contact, and
   encouragement.

2. Build the level of trust with
   the offender through empathic
   statements, eye contact, and
   encouragement.

3. Evaluate the offender's childhood history for experiences
   of physical, sexual, or emotional abuse; work at a pace
   that is not affectively overwhelming for the offender.

4. Explore how the offender may
   have internalized the behavior
   patterns of her own abuser and
   is now acting out her own abusive history.

5. Explore the offender's feelings of powerlessness that she felt as a child victim of abuse.

3. Identify the impact of being forced to cope with adult-type responsibilities while still a child. (6)

6. Explore experiences in the offender's childhood in which she was required to do tasks that were inappropriate for her age (e.g., become the lover at age 13 of a 40-year-old man, take over the household and care for younger siblings at age 10, work at a job to provide food for the family, adjust to chronic homelessness, provide care for a drug-abusing parent); probe how these experiences have shaped her attitudes about herself and children.

4. Identify the emotional needs met by sexually abusive behavior. (7)

7. Explore the offender's distorted beliefs about relationships, children, and sexuality, identifying what emotional needs are attempted to be met through sexual abuse of others.

5. Cooperate with a psychological/psychosexual evaluation, and comply with recommendations for treatment. (8)

8. Access the offender's depth of depression, suicide potential, anxiety, and other psychopathology along with psychosexual history and risk assessment.

6. Cooperate with an evaluation for physical disorders related to sexual behavior. (9)

9. Refer the offender to a physician for a complete physical (in particular, assessing for sexually transmitted diseases).

7. Verbalize an understanding of basic human sexuality. (10, 11)

10. Assign the offender to attend a class addressing basic human sexuality.

8. Describe the history and impact of participating in demeaning sexual experiences.
   (12, 13)

9. Disclose lesbian desires
   and any lesbian experiences.
   (14)

10. Identify and replace distorted
    thoughts regarding own child-
    hood abuse experiences. (15)

11. Assign reading material to the
    offender on human sexual de-
    velopment (e.g., *Sex Smart:
    How Your Childhood Shaped
    Your Sexual Life and What to
    Do About It* by Zoldbrod or
    *Understanding Human Sexual-
    ity* by Hyde and DeLamater).

12. Explore whether the offender
    has a history of prostitution,
    and evaluate her thoughts
    and feelings regarding these
    experiences.

13. Evaluate the offender for expe-
    riences of sadomasochistic sex
    forced upon her by a dominant
    male or female partner and the
    cognitive distortions surround-
    ing these occurrences.

14. Explore the offender's lesbian
    interest or experiences and her
    feelings surrounding the issue.

15. Examine the offender's dis-
    torted cognitions related to
    her own childhood abuse and
    how these distortions con-
    tribute to her current thinking
    errors (e.g., her abuser could
    not control his sexual im-
    pulses; the offender was highly
    sexed as a child and caused
    her abuser to abuse; sexual in-
    teractions are a natural part of
    intimacy between a parent and
    child); replace these errors in
    thinking with accurate, realis-
    tic thoughts.

11. Identify and replace cognitive distortions regarding the role of sex in the development of children. (16, 17)

12. Verbalize an understanding of the dysfunctional male relationships and feelings of insecurity that contributed to engaging in sexually assaultive behavior. (18, 19, 20)

13. Identify relationship behaviors that promote appropriate, consenting adult intimacy. (21, 22)

16. Explore the offender's thoughts regarding the emotional capabilities and appropriate role of sex in the development of children; assign the offender to write each cognitive distortion regarding children, and identify the experiences from her own past that resulted in distorted thoughts.

17. Reframe the offender's sexual abuse of a younger child as an inappropriate attempt to gain emotional intimacy.

18. Help the offender recognize her pattern of dysfunctional relationships with abusive males or females; review each of her relationships in detail.

19. Address how the offender confuses terror with excitement in destructive and dysfunctional relationships.

20. Explore with the offender how, in order to maintain the relationship with her lover, and because of fears of being alone and helpless, she consented to partici-pate in sexual assault on a victim.

21. Define for the offender the parameters of emotional intimacy between two same-age, consenting adults (e.g., trust, mutual respect, assertiveness).

22. Assign the offender to read *Getting the Love You Want* (Hendrix), and process the content.

14. Identify and implement alternative ways to feel empowered and assertive that are moral, ethical, and respectful of others. (23, 24, 25, 26)

23. Help the offender to explore and identify alternative methods of feeling power and control rather than engaging in sexual assault (e.g., learning new assertiveness behaviors, learning how to regulate uncomfortable affect, improving problem-solving skills).

24. Teach the offender assertiveness skills.

25. Refer the offender to a group that will educate and facilitate assertiveness skills via lectures, role play, and assignments.

26. Assign the offender to read books on assertiveness (e.g., *When I Say No I Feel Guilty* by Smith or *Boundaries: Where You End and I Begin* by Katherine).

15. List destructive behaviors engaged in to attempt to reduce negative affect and identify positive alternatives. (27)

27. Help the offender to find ways to cope with negative affect without resorting to negative coping activities (e.g., sexual abuse, self-mutilation, eating disorder behaviors, suicide attempts). (See the Emotional Dysregulation chapter in the Victim Issues part of this Planner.)

16. Cooperate with placement in group therapy. (28, 29)

28. Screen the offender for participation in a mixed-sex therapy group to focus on learning healthy male-female interaction skills; consider group dynamics in the placement decision.

17. Discuss feelings and experiences during incarceration, and verbalize insights gained from these experiences. (30, 31)

18. Develop a written plan for constructive action to reduce vocational distress and increase independence. (32)

19. Verbalize an increased understanding of how feelings of helplessness and dependency have led to poor life choices and subsequent sexual abuse/assault. (33)

20. Verbalize a commitment to a positive lifestyle that has as its goal to protect children and respect self and the rights of others. (34, 35)

29. Reinforce with the offender the group rules regarding no fraternization outside the group and no dysfunctional alliances during the group.

30. Empathize with the offender regarding rejection by her family during incarceration, few or no visitors on visiting day, and feelings about her own children in foster care.

31. Address the offender's traumatic experiences during incarceration (e.g., body searches in prison can reactivate posttraumatic stress disorder symptoms).

32. Refer the offender to a vocational counselor or job coach in order to enhance her financial independence, improve her sense of confidence, and avoid being dependent on a man for financial support.

33. Discuss feelings of helplessness, powerlessness, and how these feelings have influenced relationship choices, leading to current criminal charges.

34. Teach the offender the importance of making more responsible, healthy choices (e.g., choose a partner who is respectful; apply for jobs that are adequate to support herself; refrain from prostitution); outline steps to make each choice possible.

35. Construct a model with the offender of an abuse-free
lifestyle, including ways to
meet emotional needs and regulate affect that are not self-
destructive.

—. _____   —. _____
   _____   _____

—. _____   —. _____
   _____   _____

—. _____   —. _____
   _____   _____

DIAGNOSTIC SUGGESTIONS:

ICD-9-CM	ICD-10-CM	DSM-5 Disorder, Condition, or Problem
305.00	F10.10	Alcohol Use Disorder, Mild
303.90	F10.20	Alcohol Use Disorder, Moderate or Severe
296.xx	F31.xx	Bipolar I Disorder
296.89	F31.81	Bipolar II Disorder
311	F32.9	Unspecified Depressive Disorder
311	F32.8	Other Specified Depressive Disorder
309.81	F43.10	Posttraumatic Stress Disorder
300.14	F44.81	Dissociative Identity Disorder
301.50	F60.4	Histrionic Personality Disorder
301.83	F60.3	Borderline Personality Disorder
301.6	F60.7	Dependent Personality Disorder
301.9	F60.9	Unspecified Personality Disorder
___	___	_____
___	___	_____

GUILT/SHAME

BEHAVIORAL DEFINITIONS

1. Expresses deep feelings of shame regarding self.
2. Confuses guilt over a specific sexual offense with shame about self; sees self as worthless and depraved.
3. Sees self as unable to change actions because of serious personal inadequacies.
4. Avoids social relationships because of a deep-seated sense of shame about self.
5. Feels powerless over deviant arousal, relapse, or change in sexual focus because of overwhelming inadequacies as a person.

___. _____
    _____
    _____
___. _____
    _____
    _____
___. _____
    _____

LONG-TERM GOALS

1. Decrease self-deprecating thoughts that result in feelings of powerlessness and hopelessness.
2. Separate crime and the criminal act from the person, therefore viewing self as able to change, but taking responsibility for reprehensible actions.
3. Acknowledge that a potential relapse to offending behavior is due to changeable, controllable internal factors rather than *global self-devaluation*.

4. See self as worthy of deserving love and support, at the same time expressing and feeling remorse for the pain and violation of victim(s).

5. Use appropriate guilt to promote own moral behavior, to inhibit socially undesirable and sexually abusive behaviors, and to motivate self to do reparative actions.

__. _____
   _____

__. _____
   _____

__. _____
   _____

SHORT-TERM OBJECTIVES

THERAPEUTIC INTERVENTIONS

1. Verbalize any feelings of guilt and shame, as well as the origin of these feelings. (1)

2. Verbalize an understanding of the distinction between appropriate guilt for an immoral act and shame about self. (2, 3)

1. Express empathy for the offender's feelings of shame and guilt.

2. Explain to the offender that shame is a painful focus on the devalued self that is often accompanied by feelings of powerlessness, worthlessness, and insignificance. Shame tends to make a person withdraw from others. (See "Conceptual and Methodological Issues in the Assessment of Shame and Guilt" by Tagney in *Behavior Research and Therapy.*)

3. Explain to the offender that guilt is the affective response that results when you perceive that you have violated a moral standard by your actions. (See "Conceptual and Methodological Issues in the Assessment of

Shame and Guilt" by Tagney in *Behavior Research and Therapy*.)

3. Identify the relationship between how significant family members modeled shame and guilt for the offender in childhood and own shame and guilt felt currently. (4)

4. Explore with the offender, through a genogram and discussion, his/her feelings of guilt and shame and how they are related to experiences with early-life caretakers (parents); discuss how these experiences influenced his/her view of guilt and shame.

4. Verbalize an appropriate sense of guilt regarding sexually abusive/assaultive behaviors. (3, 5, 6)

3. Explain to the offender that guilt is the affective response that results when you perceive that you have violated a moral standard by your actions. (See "Conceptual and Methodological Issues in the Assessment of Shame and Guilt" by Tagney in *Behavior Research and Therapy*.)

5. Assign the offender to write an apology letter (unsent), expressing guilt and accepting responsibility for the abusive acts; ask him/her to read the letter to the therapist or the therapy group.

6. Reflect back to the offender his/her words and thoughts about guilt, shame regarding the offense, and other actions in his/her life. Challenge his/her misperceptions, rationalizations, denial, and shame-based self-talk.

5. Verbalize a decrease in viewing self as powerless, and replace with a belief in the ability to change and have feelings of self-efficacy. (7, 8)

6. Write a letter to self, admitting the actions of manipulating and coercing the victim(s), and taking responsibility for action without devaluing himself/herself. (9, 10)

7. Assist the offender in understanding that shame-free guilt is correlated with both the perception that relationships can be positive, as well as with the ability to manage anger appropriately and empathize with others. (See *Cognitive Behavioral Treatment of Sexual Offenders* by Marshall, Anderson, and Fernandez.)

8. Discuss with the offender how to distinguish between himself/herself as bad, and behavior as bad; use abuse behaviors along with other more common illegal behaviors (e.g., speeding, cheating on tax returns, underreporting earned tips) as examples of *bad behavior* that can be distinguished from a *bad person*.

9. Assign the offender to write an account of his/her sexual crime(s) and to confront any denial regarding responsibility for his/her actions.

10. Assist the offender in listing specific actions of manipulation and coercion used with victims (e.g., offering attention to a needy child, implying physical threats, using alcohol or drugs to lower resistance) and verbalizing appropriate guilt, but not shame.

7. Verbalize an understanding of the effects of sexual assault on victims. (11)

8. Write an apology letter (unsent) to the victim's family acknowledging guilt for actions of sexual abuse/assault. (12)

9. Express empathy for the victim of sexual assault. (11, 12, 13)

11. Assist the offender in listing the effect that his/her sexual assault has had on the victim(s) (e.g., fear, hypersexuality, low self-esteem, distrust of others, inappropriate guilt).

12. Assign the offender to write an apology letter to the victim's family; ask the offender to read this apology letter aloud, challeng-ing his/her denial and minimization.

11. Assist the offender in listing the effect that his/her sexual assault has had on the victim(s) (e.g., fear, hypersexuality, low self-esteem, distrust of others, inappropriate guilt).

12. Assign the offender to write an apology letter to the victim's family; ask the offender to read this apology letter aloud, challeng-ing his/her denial and minimization.

13. Assign the offender to read about (or visit the site if within the conditions mandated by probation/parole) disasters or other large-scale tragedies and their memorials (e.g., Holocaust Museum, 9-11 Memorial, Vietnam War Memorial) and discuss the emotional impact to the victims, their families, and society in general; compare this large-scale suffering to the serious suffering of his/her victim(s).

10. Make a commitment to be a positive force in society by altruistic contributions to society. (14)

11. Identify and replace distorted self-talk that promotes shame. (15, 16)

12. Identify how using guilt as a signal for behavioral change could positively impact own life and others. (17, 18)

14. Assist the offender in making a list of actions that he/she can perform that will be of service to the community [e.g., maintaining his/her own relapse prevention plan, treating others with respect and kindness, taking monetary responsibilities for all financial costs that resulted from his/her crime (e.g., paying for the victim's therapy)].

15. Probe distorted automatic thoughts that trigger shame in different situations (e.g., when making mistakes, being assertive, asking for help); replace distorted thoughts with realistic, positive self-talk.

16. Have the offender identify adjectives or phrases that he/she uses to devalue himself/herself (*self-disgust; self-contempt;* "I was horrified at myself," rather than "I was horrified at what I had done"); replace distorted cognitions with realistic thoughts.

17. Assist the offender in identifying victim grooming behaviors (performing special favors for the victim, giving inappropriate gifts, giving special attention) that lead to guilt feelings (which were ignored) before the offense.

18. Assign the offender to discuss with the therapist or group how his/her behavior would

have changed if he/she had listened to and reacted appropriately to the guilt feelings before the crime.

13. Report improved self-esteem and knowledge about how thoughts influence feelings. (19, 20)

19. Use specific cognitive-behavioral strategies to build self-esteem. (See the Self-Esteem Deficit chapter in the Offender and Victim part of this Planner.)

20. Assign the offender to read *Feeling Good: The New Mood Therapy* (Burns); process how thoughts impact feelings.

14. Identify situations where other immoral behavior has been implemented, and describe the consequences to self and others. (21)

21. Ask the offender to identify past immoral behaviors (e.g., stealing from a family member, lying to a spouse, drug abuse) and the negative impact on himself/herself and others (e.g., relationship loss, self-esteem loss, depression).

15. Verbalize an understanding that shame is pervasive and destructive to self-esteem. (22, 23)

22. Assist the offender in developing an awareness of his/her patterns of shame-based attributions in everyday life (e.g., "no one could ever love me because of what I did"; "I'm worthless"; "I don't deserve to ask for what I need"). (See *Cognitive Behavioral Treatment of Sexual Offenders* by Marshall, Anderson, and Fernandez.)

23. Teach the offender how shame has become a part of his/her self-concept, has resulted in a view of himself/herself as a grossly inadequate person, and how this is a very painful way to live.

16. Identify shame triggers and develop strategies for constructively dealing with each trigger. (24)

24. Help the offender explore shame triggers (e.g., being the target of anger from another person, being rejected by a significant other, being questioned about the sexual offense by an authority figure or law enforcement official) by keeping a daily record of shame thoughts and using positive replacement thoughts about himself/herself to reduce feelings of shame.

17. Articulate a commitment to use guilt as an emotional signal to evaluate behavior, to let go of shame, and to not allow thoughts of global self-devaluation to take control of life. (25)

25. Assign the offender to develop and process a written life plan that outlines a moral lifestyle, using guilt as a signal to evaluate behavior and learning how to release shame to avoid global self-devaluation. (See *Cognitive Behavioral Treatment of Sexual Offenders* by Marshall, Anderson, and Fernandez.)

___. _____
_____
___. _____
_____
___. _____
_____

___. _____
_____
___. _____
_____
___. _____
_____

DIAGNOSTIC SUGGESTIONS:

ICD-9-CM	ICD-10-CM	DSM-5 Disorder, Condition, or Problem
300.4	F34.1	Persistent Depressive Disorder
296.xx	F32.x	Major Depressive Disorder, Single Episode
296.xx	F33.x	Major Depressive Disorder, Recurrent Episode
300.02	F41.1	Generalized Anxiety Disorder
301.9	F60.9	Unspecified Personality Disorder
_____	_____	_____
_____	_____	_____

LEGAL ISSUES

BEHAVIORAL DEFINITIONS

1. Legal pressure has been central to the decision to enter treatment for sexual offending.
2. Sexual offenses have resulted in arrest and/or incarceration.
3. Legal charges for sexual offending are pending.
4. Fear of loss of freedom due to current sexual offense charges.
5. Separation or divorce proceedings are pending, accompanied by emotional turmoil.
6. Probation is subsequent to sexual offense charges.
7. History of incarceration and parole for sexual abuse.
8. Chemical dependence has resulted in several arrests and current court involvement.

__. _____

_____

__. _____

_____

__. _____

_____

LONG-TERM GOALS

1. Accept and responsibly respond to the mandates of the court.
2. Accept responsibility for the sexual behavior that resulted in the legal charge and conviction.
3. Accept the need for treatment to change values, thoughts, feelings, and behavior to a more prosocial position.

4. Accept and adapt to the uncontrollable actions of the court.
5. Develop higher moral and ethical standards to govern behavior.

__. _____
_____

__. _____
_____

__. _____
_____

SHORT-TERM OBJECTIVES

THERAPEUTIC INTERVENTIONS

1. Identify the sexual behaviors that led to the current involvement with the court system. (1, 2)

1. Explore the offender's perception of the sexual behaviors that led to legal charges; clarify if treatment is court-mandated and required to be focused only on sexual offenses, or to include issues such as substance abuse treatment.

2. Clarify payment arrangements for treatment, and ask the offender to sign a financial agreement and appropriate release(s) of information; verify that he/she has a clear understanding of the limits of confidentiality.

2. Cooperate with legally required treatment, giving permission for disclosure of treatment status and progress to any agencies involved. (3, 4)

3. Clarify the involvement of the probation/parole officer as part of the treatment team, and identify the nature and frequency of treatment information that must be reported.

4. Clarify the involvement of social services or child

protective services as to the nature and amount of treatment information to be shared.

3. Express feelings toward the legal system in an appropriate manner. (5)

5. Explore the impact that the process of adjudication has had on the offender's life and emotions.

4. Verbalize an understanding and acceptance of the rules surrounding treatment compliance. (6, 7)

6. Clarify the consequences of treatment noncompliance (e.g., missed sessions, refusal to turn in homework assignments, oppositionality).

7. Clarify with the court/probation/parole agents relevant collaborative treatment issues (e.g., ability of offender to make unilateral decisions regarding change in treatment providers, family reunification procedures, responsibility of payment).

5. Verbalize an understanding of the limits of confidentiality. (8)

8. Explain and clarify the limits of confidentiality regarding information from the therapy session before the offender gives written consent for sharing information with others; explore how the reduction in confidentiality may affect his/her openness in sessions.

6. List circumstances and situations that must be avoided as part of the probation/parole and treatment. (9)

9. Help the offender to confront and accept the reality that because he/she has been convicted of sexual assault/abuse, he/she is vulnerable to the misinterpretation of his/her behavior in the future; teach him/her the need to avoid

7. Verbalize the long- and short-term consequences of the criminal offenses. (10)

8. Verbalize an understanding of the reasons, mandated by probation/parole and supported by the treatment contract, for restrictions from use of pornographic materials. (11)

9. Disclose any travel plans to the probation/parole officer, requesting permission and complying with the response to the request. (12)

10. List the requirements of Megan's law regarding registration of residence and travel restrictions. (13, 14)

some situations not only to decrease the danger of relapse, but also to protect himself/herself from the vulnerability of future accusations due to a perception of guilt.

10. Help the offender to list the direct legal consequences of his/her crime (e.g., loss of the privilege of voting, loss of the right of unrestricted travel, the requirement to be listed in a state sex offender registry).

11. Explain to the offender the reasons that use of adult pornography is not permitted (e.g., adult pornography use can contribute to sexual addiction; pornography use can bolster sexual preoccupation; pornography can be used to fuel deviant fantasies).

12. Help the offender to make realistic travel plans, and encourage him/her to voice frustrations regarding legal restrictions on travel as an alternative to acting out.

13. Review the state laws regarding sex offender travels and the requirements for registration (e.g., how many days the offender may stay in the state without registering and the consequences for not abiding by state laws).

11. Acknowledge guilt in committing a sexual offense. (15)

12. Outline a plan for a job search, including employment restrictions and consultation with the probation/parole officer. (16)

13. Identify how substance abuse led to current charges/convictions, and sign an abstinence contract. (17)

14. Comply with the probation/parole contract, cooperating with and keeping contact with the officer. (18, 19, 20)

14. Explore the offender's re-sistance to and denial of problems associated with Megan's law requirements; assign him/her to investigate the state laws re- garding registration of residence.

15. Request a transcript of the trial proceedings in which the offender admitted guilt, and use it in treatment to confront denial.

16. Help the offender to develop a written job plan that contains specific, attainable objectives for a job search and includes restrictions mandated by the probation/parole officer (e.g., em-ployer notification of being on probation/parole, no contact with children, travel restrictions).

17. Explore the offender's chemical dependence as to its contribution to previous arrests and current court involvement; develop an abstinence contract to be signed by the offender. (See the Substance Abuse chapter in the Offender and Victim Issues part of this Planner.)

18. Review the terms and conditions of the offender's probation/parole contract.

19. Explain to the offender that treatment is a collabor-ative venture between the therapist and the probation/parole

officer and that there will be frequent and detailed communication between the officer and the therapist.

20. Explain that treatment includes multidisciplinary collaboration between the therapist, the probation/parole officer, the court, child protective services, and other agencies and individuals involved in treatment or adjudication.

15. Verbalize and accept the restrictions on sexually related behavior that have resulted from illegal actions. (21)

21. Contact the probation/parole officer regarding the results of examining the offender's place of living for pornography, sexually related items, pictures of children, and computer activities.

16. Verbalize feelings of shame and embarrassment regarding the probation/parole officer making home visits. (22)

22. Explore the offender's feelings of being intruded upon due to the probation/parole officer performing home visits; address the fear of being exposed to the neighbors as a sex offender.

17. Verbalize feelings of fear and shame related to public notification of the community regarding the whereabouts of sex offenders in their community. (23)

23. Explore the offender's fears regarding vigilantism and feelings of shame regarding public or Internet notification of his/her place of residence; refer the offender to his/her probation/parole officer to discuss the issue of harassment by his/her neighbors and the remediation measures that are available.

18. Disclose prison experiences and the mandates of prison culture. (24, 25)

24. Ask the offender to talk about his/her experiences in prison; encourage exploration of the issue of the offender not having control in prison, anger toward the prison system, and problems with the guards and other prisoners.

25. Assist the offender in discussing the difficulties associated with being a sex offender in prison (e.g., having to avoid any appearance of weakness because of the consequences of showing vulnerability, fear of being revealed as a sex offender, suffering brutalization from other inmates).

19. Identify feelings stemming from past prison experience. (26)

26. Assign the offender to construct a role play of his/her prison experience with other group members in order to experience emotions that have been avoided or denied.

20. Family members identify their behaviors that impede the offender's compliance with the probation/parole contract. (27)

27. Help the offender's spouse and other family members to identify their own be-haviors that have not supported the offender's compliance with the probation/parole contract and that could have resulted in a technical violation leading to incarceration (e.g., demanding that the offender travel out of state for an important family function without getting per-

mission from the probation/parole officer, leaving children in the care of the offender for even a short period of time, refusing to attend family therapy).

21. Family members express their feelings regarding the terms of the offender's probation/parole contract that impact their lives. (28, 29)

28. Explore how the family members feel about the offender's probation officer driving up to him/her in a police car for all the neighbors to see at unpredictable times to initiate home searches.

29. Assist the offender's partner in developing coping mechanisms to deal with the conflicted feelings surrounding the intrusion of the court and the probation/parole officer in the home.

22. Identify feelings regarding the pending separation or divorce. (30)

30. Explore the offender's feelings regarding the pending separation or divorce and the accompanying emotional turmoil of the entire family.

23. Partner attend a nonoffending partner psychoeducational support group. (31)

31. Refer the offender's partner to a nonoffending partner group focused on coping with issues of stress within the sex offender's family. (See a model presented in *Treating Nonoffending Parents in Child Sexual Abuse Cases: Connections for Family Safety* by Levenson and Morin.)

—. _____   —. _____
    _____   _____
—. _____   —. _____
    _____   _____
—. _____   —. _____
    _____   _____

DIAGNOSTIC SUGGESTIONS:

ICD-9-CM	ICD-10-CM	DSM-5 Disorder, Condition, or Problem
300.4	F34.1	Persistent Depressive Disorder
296.xx	F32.x	Major Depressive Disorder, Single Episode
296.xx	F33.x	Major Depressive Disorder, Recurrent Episode
300.02	F41.1	Generalized Anxiety Disorder
312.34	F63.81	Intermittent Explosive Disorder
303.90	F10.20	Alcohol Use Disorder, Moderate or Severe
305.00	F10.10	Alcohol Use Disorder, Mild
304.30	F12.20	Cannabis Use Disorder, Moderate or Severe
305.20	F12.10	Cannabis Use Disorder, Mild
304.20	F14.20	Cocaine Use Disorder, Moderate or Severe
305.60	F14.10	Cocaine Use Disorder, Mild
305.70	F15.10	Amphetamine Use Disorder, Mild
304.40	F15.20	Amphetamine Use Disorder, Moderate or Severe
305.50	F11.10	Opioid Use Disorder, Mild
304.00	F11.20	Opioid Use Disorder, Moderate or Severe
305.90	F18.10	Inhalant Use Disorder, Mild
304.60	F18.20	Inhalant Use Disorder, Moderate or Severe
301.9	F60.9	Unspecified Personality Disorder
301.7	F60.2	Antisocial Personality Disorder

RELAPSE PREVENTION

BEHAVIORAL DEFINITIONS

1. A history of repeatedly committing sexual abuse offenses.
2. Previous attempts at treatment have resulted in relapse.
3. Engages in high-risk trigger behaviors (e.g., reading or viewing pornography, chatting with children on the Internet, befriending needy children, following or spending time alone with potential targets of abuse/assault).
4. Verbalizes denial of responsibility for negative consequences of the sexual abuse/assault.
5. Expresses doubt regarding the ability to control the sexual urges and deviant behavior.
6. A history of terminating treatment and avoiding contact with a positive support system.
7. Lacks social skills and is quite isolated.
8. Has recently expressed interest in and strong motivation for treatment to terminate the sexual offense cycle.
9. A chronic pattern of periods of control over deviant sexual impulses followed by relapse into sexual abuse.

__. _____

   _____

__. _____

   _____

__. _____

   _____

LONG-TERM GOALS

1. Understand the concept of relapse prevention and how it pertains to sex offenses and the sexual assault cycle.
2. Understand own sexual assault cycle by identifying behaviors, thoughts, feelings, and situations that are high-risk precursors to offending.
3. Develop and implement a relapse prevention plan that is supported by the therapist, spouse, family, and probation/parole officer.
4. Identify high-risk situations, internal and external deterrents to relapse, and responsible living behaviors.

—. _____
   _____
—. _____
   _____
—. _____
   _____

SHORT-TERM OBJECTIVES

1. Verbalize a belief in own ability to change behavior and disrupt the sexual assault cycle. (1, 2)

2. Verbalize an understanding that relapse prevention is a method designed to help offenders learn self-control and strategies to maintain offense-free lives. (3)

THERAPEUTIC INTERVENTIONS

1. Explore the offender's belief in his/her ability to stop his/her sexual assault cycle; replace negative self-talk with positive cognitions regarding his/her own capabilities.

2. Express compassion for the offender, and encourage the development of trust between the offender and therapist.

3. Present to the offender the components of the relapse prevention model [e.g., seemingly unimportant decision (SUD), abstinence violation effect (AVE), lapse]

3. Describe own offense cycle in an honest and genuine manner, including thoughts, feelings, behaviors, and defenses. (4, 5, 6, 7)

4. Identify distorted beliefs and fantasies that support sexually assaultive/abusive behavior. (8, 9)

as presented in *Handbook for Sexual Abuser Assessment and Treatment* (Carich and Mussack, eds.).

4. Assign the offender to write a narrative description of the abuse, how he/she chose the victim, groomed the victim, got the victim alone, and so forth.

5. Explore with the offender each step in the offense process: deviant fantasies and beliefs entertained; what he/she did to select, groom, and isolate the victim; what his/her thoughts and feelings were during each step; and how denial is used.

6. Explore the offender's guilt and other negative affect experienced after the offense and what dysfunctional defenses he/she used to escape these uncomfortable feelings (e.g., having more deviant fantasies, daydreaming about feeling powerful, blaming the victim for the offense).

7. Explore the offender's promises to himself/herself after the assault that he/she "will never do it again"; explain how this is a form of denial and minimization.

8. Assign the offender to list the personal and social obstacles that he/she had to overcome to commit the offense (e.g., personal conscience, fear of incarceration for offense, suffering of the victim); process the list to identify

5. Identify 10 personal risk factors that increase the likelihood of offending. (10, 11)

dysfunctional thoughts and beliefs that are used to escape the obstacles.

9. Explore the offender's deviant fantasies and beliefs that support and precipitate his/her sexually assaultive behavior. (See the Deviant Sexual Arousal chapter in the Offender Issues part of this Planner.)

10. Assign the offender to construct a written account of his/her relapse cycle (e.g., victim selection; victim grooming; own thoughts, beliefs, feelings, and defenses) to present to the therapist and/or group; during a review, identify his/her personal triggers for relapse. (See *Cognitive Behavioral Treatment for Sexual Offenders* by Marshall, Anderson, and Fernandez.)

11. Assist the offender in identifying *thoughts* (e.g., "I'm worthless"; "No one loves me"; "Most women want to be forced to have sex"), *feelings* (e.g., anger, loneliness, guilt), and *actions* (e.g., getting an apartment across the street from a school, viewing pornography on the Internet, drinking alcohol) that are risks or triggers that can lead to his/her relapse.

6. Explain how loneliness, anger, frustration, a need for power and control, or rejection by others could lead to an increased risk of sexual offense. (12)

7. List escape or avoidance strategies for each risk factor that will interrupt the progression to a sexual offense. (13, 14, 15, 16)

8. Implement the carrying of three-by-five-inch cards that state avoidance and escape strategies. (17)

12. Have the offender complete exercises from Chapter 4 in *Facing the Shadow* (Schwartz and Canfield) to learn how emotions influence relapse.

13. Have the offender identify avoidance strategies (e.g., never babysitting a child, not picking up hitchhikers, maintaining sobriety) that reduce the risk of relapse.

14. Have the offender identify escape strategies (e.g., leave a party where drugs are being passed around, leave the room when someone turns on a pornographic movie, walk out of an adult bookstore) that reduce the risk of relapse.

15. For each of the offender's risk factors, have him/her list two specific escape and two specific avoidance strategies.

16. Assist the offender in developing escape and avoidance strategies that are particular to his/her sexual assault cycle (e.g., child molester—avoid socializing with women who have minor children; exhibitionist—never drive alone in a car; rapist—avoid possession of articles used in past rapes such as rope, tape, etc.).

17. Instruct the offender to print or type five general escape and five general avoidance strategies on a three-by-five-inch card and put it in his/her wallet; ask him/her to read the cards once daily in order to

9. Acknowledge responsibility for and list the negative consequences to self and others of not controlling own sexual behavior. (18, 19)

10. Identify support individuals who will not facilitate deviant behaviors but will be available to assist in preventing relapse. (20, 21)

11. Verbalize an understanding that family members and court officials must be informed of the relapse prevention plan. (22, 23)

remind himself/herself of options. (See *Handbook for Sexual Abuser Assessment and Treatment* by Carich and Mussack.)

18. Require the offender to verbalize responsibility for the assault, detailing the consequences to the victim and to himself/herself.

19. Teach the offender that he/she is still responsible for his/her sexually abusive behavior, even though he/she committed the offense while choosing to be under the influence of a mood-altering substance.

20. Teach the offender how a support system can be helpful in reducing relapse risk (e.g., assist in maintaining sobriety, meet emotional intimacy needs, help monitor and point out dysfunctional behaviors).

21. Use role playing and modeling to teach the offender how to ask others for support when in a difficult situation that may lead to relapse.

22. Consult with the offender's probation/parole officer regarding the specifics of the relapse prevention plan; point out environments and people who must be avoided.

23. Fully inform the offender's family members regarding the relapse prevention plan; point out environments and people who must be avoided.

12. Define physical contact and intimacy boundaries for healthy, respectful interpersonal relationships. (24, 25, 26)

24. Assign the offender to read a book about intimacy boundaries (e.g., *Where to Draw the Line* by Katherine); process key concepts.

25. Help the offender to define and list appropriate and inappropriate social touching (e.g., shaking hands, touching the elbow, giving high fives), verbal remarks (e.g., no sexual innuendoes, no lewd or suggestive comments), and physical gestures (e.g., no suggestive or lewd acts, no displays of private parts, no fondling or groping); solicit group and significant-other feedback.

26. Explore the offender's personal and family history of physical contact, including personal abuse history; identify appropriate and inappropriate boundaries for touching.

13. Implement stress management strategies to reduce the risk for relapse. (27)

27. Teach the offender about stress management and how those skills can help to prevent relapse (e.g., establish a structured daily schedule). (See the Stress Management Deficits chapter in the Offender and Victim Issues part of this Planner.)

14. Identify fears and frustrations regarding treatment. (28)

28. Explore the offender's views and frustrations about treatment; acknowledge his/her fears about loss of control and fears of intimacy.

15. Initiate constructive and safe community-based activities. (29)

29. Assist the offender in identifying appropriate and safe ways to contribute to the community (participating in a restorative justice program, committing to attending religious services regularly, volunteering a service to an appropriate charity); solicit an agreement to initiate such activity.

16. Develop an aftercare plan that includes treatment, social support system, and relapse prevention plan. (30, 31)

30. Help the offender to develop an aftercare plan that includes treatment, social support, and relapse prevention, discussing the availability of appropriate community resources and problem-solving impediments to staying safe; communicate this plan to significant others. (See *Handbook for Sexual Abuser Assessment and Treatment* by Carich and Mussack.)

31. Give the offender a referral for specific resources for support groups (e.g., Alcoholics Anonymous, Sexaholics Anonymous, Families United).

17. Participate in drama therapy, role-playing high-risk situations that could lead to relapse. (32)

32. Role-play with the offender high-risk situations that could occur in the future, modeling resolution (e.g., being asked to baby-sit for a child in an emergency situation, spending extended time with a close family member who is in denial of the offender's crime, viewing a pornographic movie at a party, attending church and being asked to help with the children's service at church); process his/her feelings.

18. Identify the rewards that are as-
    sociated with maintaining con-
    trol over sexual behavior. (33)

33. Ask the offender to list the
    positive, long-term benefits to
    himself/herself, to potential
    victims, and to society of de-
    veloping and practicing a life-
    long relapse prevention plan.

__. _____

__. _____

__. _____

__. _____

__. _____

__. _____

DIAGNOSTIC SUGGESTIONS:

ICD-9-CM	_ICD-10-CM_	_DSM-5_ Disorder, Condition, or Problem
302.4	F65.2	Exhibitionistic Disorder
302.81	F65.0	Fetishistic Disorder
302.89	F65.81	Frotteuristic Disorder
302.2	F65.4	Pedophilic Disorder
302.83	F65.51	Sexual Masochism Disorder
302.84	F65.52	Sexual Sadism Disorder
302.82	F65.3	Voyeuristic Disorder
302.89	F65.9	Unspecified Paraphilic Disorder
_____	_____	_____
_____	_____	_____

RELATIONSHIP SKILLS DEFICITS

BEHAVIORAL DEFINITIONS

1. Pattern of high social anxiety, social ineptness, social isolation and loneliness, low self-confidence in social situations, and frequent feelings of jealousy.
2. Lacks the ability and/or confidence to initiate or maintain conversations with others.
3. Poor skills at recognizing and identifying with the emotions of others.
4. Does not recognize and identify with the emotions of others.
5. Misinterprets a partner's level of interest in sexuality, mistaking friendly behavior for seduction.
6. A pattern of repeated broken or conflictual relationships due to personal deficiencies in problem-solving and maintaining a trust relationship.
7. Avoids closeness with a partner through maintaining a pattern of superficial or no communication, infrequent or no sexual contact, excessive involvement in activities (work or recreation).
8. Initiates physical and/or verbal abuse in a relationship.
9. Involvement in multiple intimate relationships at the same time with no emotional connection to partners.

___. _____
_____

___. _____
_____

___. _____
_____

LONG-TERM GOALS

1. Develop effective social skills that will meet intimacy needs and enhance quality of life.
2. Increase confidence in social competence.
3. Develop the necessary skills for effective, open communication, mutually satisfying sexual intimacy, and enjoyable time for companionship within the relationship.
4. Make a commitment to one intimate relationship at a time.

__. _____

_____

__. _____

_____

__. _____

_____

SHORT-TERM OBJECTIVES	THERAPEUTIC INTERVENTIONS
1. Identify and clarify the nature of social skills and relationship deficits. (1, 2)	1. Assist the offender in identifying how aspects of his/her interpersonal style decrease the chance for intimate relationships.
	2. Interpret how the lack of closeness in the offender's relationships results in negative affect and can lead to seeking an inappropriate sexual contact or relapse.
2. Identify the emotional detachment that existed in the family and the consequences of this experience. (3, 4)	3. Explore the offender's family history of dysfunctional relationship styles.
	4. Explore the offender's emotional reaction (e.g., feeling unloved, isolated) to the dysfunctional, detached

3. Identify negative self-talk that increases social anxiety and leads to social avoidance and isolation. (5)

4. Complete a social anxiety rating scale, and discuss specific areas where anxiety is particularly high. (6)

5. Cooperate with a referral to a physician for an evaluation for antianxiety medication. (7, 8)

6. Initiate and maintain at least one social interaction daily. (9, 10)

relationships that existed within his/her family.

5. Assist the offender in identifying negative thinking about himself/herself that leads to social anxiety and withdrawal.

6. Administer a social anxiety assessment instrument (e.g., Leibowitz Social Anxiety Scale or the Social Phobia Inventory) to the offender and discuss areas of high social discomfort.

7. Evaluate the offender for the need for medication to ameliorate anxiety symptoms, and arrange for a psychiatric evaluation, if necessary.

8. Monitor the offender for medication compliance, effectiveness, and side effects; consult with the prescribing physician, if necessary.

9. Assign the offender to initiate one conversation daily, increasing time from one to five minutes per interaction, and report the results to the therapist.

10. Role-play difficult social situations with the offender (e.g., asking for help with a problem at work, disagreeing with a friend, asking for feedback from a friend about a mutual interaction) to help remove obstacles to social interaction.

7. Acknowledge that engaging in impersonal sexual encounters is an attempt to satisfy intimacy needs. (11, 12)

11. Explore the offender's history of substituting impersonal sexual encounters for genuine intimate relationships; confront denial regarding impersonal sexual relationships and acts of abuse/assault.

12. Assist the offender in understanding how a manipulated, forced, or coerced sexual act is not intimacy, but that it results in emotional damage.

8. Acknowledge that denial of the importance of intimacy is a way to protect self from getting hurt or rejected by others. (13)

13. Help the offender to explore his/her history of physical, emotional, and sexual abuse and how that may have led to mistrust of others and avoidance of the vulnerability of intimacy.

9. Verbalize the feelings that are associated with being socially isolated. (14)

14. Explore with the offender his/her experience of not being in a relationship and how that isolation may lead to increased negative self-talk about being substandard and worthless.

10. Make a list of positive coping strategies to deal with loneliness. (15)

15. Teach effective strategies (e.g., develop a support system; have a list of friends to call when feeling lonely; volunteer at an appropriately supervised adult activity to benefit society) for dealing with loneliness as alternatives to relapse.

11. Identify the positive aspects of being alone, and spend 10 minutes each day alone, enjoying the time. (16, 17)

16. Challenge the offender's distorted negative thinking about being alone; substitute with positive thoughts regarding being alone.

17. Assign the offender to keep a daily journal recording the times spent alone and the feelings experienced.

12. Acknowledge feelings of jealousy and the impact that they have had. (18, 19, 20)

18. Teach the offender how jealousy results from low self-esteem, fear of rejection, and a personal history of unfaithfulness.

19. Ask the offender to make a list of the ways in which jealousy has negatively impacted his/her life; process this list. (See *Cognitive Behavioral Treatment of Sexual Offenders* by Marshall, Anderson and Fernandez.)

20. Probe the offender's fear of being hurt and rejected by others; explore how this leads to avoidance of relationships and subsequent jealousy. (See *Cognitive Behavioral Treatment of Sexual Offenders* by Marshall, Anderson and Fernandez.)

13. Identify ways to deal with jealousy when it occurs. (21)

21. Assign the offender to make a list of coping skills that he/she can use when jealous feelings occur (e.g., checking for feelings of personal inadequacy, exploring any cognitive distortions, entertaining alternate explanations of others' words and actions). (See *Cognitive Behavioral Treatment of Sexual Offenders* by Marshall, Anderson, and Fernandez.)

14. Identify instances of inappropriate anger at others because of mistrust and fear of rejection. (22, 23)

15. Practice relating to others in an empathic manner in daily living. (24)

16. Verbalize an understanding that self-acceptance is an essential part of the ability to feel empathy for others and prevent relapse. (25)

17. Increase the frequency of self-disclosure by practicing daily. (26)

18. Decrease sensitivity to rejection in relationships by identifying and replacing negative self-talk that occurs when rejection is experienced. (27, 28)

22. Assist the offender in identifying instances when he/she became angry at someone due to mistrust or fear of rejection.

23. Teach the offender more effective ways to cope with anger. (See the Anger Difficulties chapter in the Offender Issues part of this Planner.)

24. Assist the offender in developing an awareness of the feelings of others by using role play and modeling of empathic understanding. (See the Empathy Deficits chapter in the Offender Issues part of this Planner.)

25. Assign the offender to talk positively about himself/ herself while facing a mirror and practice this self-acceptance exercise twice daily; emphasize the importance of self-acceptance as a prerequisite to empathy for others.

26. Model for the offender appropriate self-disclosure in role play in session, and encourage him/her to increase his/her self-disclosure to trusted others.

27. Explore with the offender feelings of rejection related to early family relationships, and relate these to distorted, negative thoughts about himself/herself when rejection occurred.

19. Explore and establish guidelines for boundaries for appropriate expression of physical affection. (29, 30)

20. Implement new conflict resolution techniques in current relationships. (31)

21. Report an increase in sexual satisfaction with the appropriate partner in a romantic relationship resulting from direct and empathic communication. (32)

28. Explore the offender's current cognitive distortions that occur when he/she perceives being rejected; replace these negative messages with positive self-talk.

29. Assign the offender to develop a list of appropriate ways to verbally express affection to others; review and process the list with proper boundaries being considered.

30. Discuss appropriate expression of physical affection in relationships, assisting the offender in how to identify clear verbal or behavioral signals from other adults regarding the degree of physical affection that is acceptable.

31. Teach the offender how to apply principles of conflict resolution to interpersonal relationships (e.g., be specific about his/her needs; improve listening skills; seek a mutually satisfying plan of action); process his/her experience at applying these principals, giving redirection where indicated.

32. Explore past or current sexual difficulties with the appropriate partner, and coach the offender on how to appropriately communicate these concerns to his/her partner.

22. Define the aspects of a healthy intimate relationship. (33, 34)

23. Acknowledge destructive patterns of intimate relationships that have led to sexual abuse offenses. (35)

33. Assist the offender in developing a list of criteria for a healthy intimate relationship (e.g., mutual respect, bilateral listening of both partners, verbal expression of affection, commitment).

34. Explore the issue of the offender's lack of commitment in relationships and his/her fears that impede commitment (e.g., fear of rejection, fear of giving up control, fear of the unknown).

35. Assist the offender in identifying dysfunctional patterns that have occurred in his/her intimate relationships (e.g., viewing his/her partner as an object to be used for sexual gratification, using force and coercion, viewing the child as an emotional-age peer).

___. _____
_____

___. _____
_____

___. _____
_____

___. _____
_____

___. _____
_____

___. _____
_____

DIAGNOSTIC SUGGESTIONS:

ICD-9-CM	_ICD-10-CM_	_DSM-5_ Disorder, Condition, or Problem
300.23	F40.10	Social Anxiety Disorder (Social Phobia)
300.4	F34.1	Persistent Depressive Disorder
300.00	F41.9	Unspecified Anxiety Disorder
301.20	F60.1	Schizoid Personality Disorder
301.81	F60.81	Narcissistic Personality Disorder
301.9	F60.9	Unspecified Personality Disorder
_____	_____	_____
_____	_____	_____

Part 3

OFFENDER AND VICTIM ISSUES

ANXIETY, PANIC, AND DEPRESSION

BEHAVIORAL DEFINITIONS

1. Excessive and persistent daily worry about several life circumstances that has no factual or logical basis, or is grossly out of proportion with reality.
2. Complains of motor tension (e.g., restlessness, tiredness, shakiness, or muscle tension).
3. A persistent and unreasonable fear of a specific object or situation that promotes avoidance behaviors because an encounter with the phobic stimulus provokes an immediate anxiety response.
4. Unexpected sudden, debilitating panic symptoms (e.g., shallow breathing, sweating, heart racing or pounding, dizziness, depersonalization or derealization, trembling, chest tightness, fear of dying or losing control, nausea) that have occurred repeatedly, resulting in persisting concern about having additional attacks or behavioral changes to avoid attacks.
5. Fear of being in an environment that may trigger intense anxiety symptoms (panic) and, therefore, avoids such situations (e.g., leaving home alone, being in a crowd of people, traveling in an enclosed environment).
6. Persistence of fear in spite of the recognition that the fear is unreasonable.
7. Experience autonomic hyperactivity (e.g., palpitations, shortness of breath, dry mouth, trouble swallowing, nausea, or diarrhea).
8. Demonstrates hypervigilance (e.g., feeling constantly on edge, concentration difficulties, and general state of irritability).
9. Feelings of dysphoria, hopelessness, worthlessness, inappropriate guilt, and/or low self-esteem.
10. Experiences loss of appetite, psychomotor retardation, sleep disturbance, lack of energy, social withdrawal, or suicidal thoughts.
11. Mood-related hallucinations or delusions.

12. Unresolved loss or grief issues, including those related to sexual abuse/assault.
13. Diminished interest in or enjoyment of activities.
14. History of chronic or recurrent depression for which antidepressant medication has been taken, and client has been hospitalized, has had outpatient treatment, or has had a course of electroconvulsive therapy.

___. _____

_____

___. _____

_____

___. _____

_____

LONG-TERM GOALS

1. Reduce overall level, frequency, and intensity of the anxiety so that daily functioning is not impaired.
2. Resolve the core conflict that is the source of anxiety.
3. Reduce fear of independently and freely leaving home to be comfortable in public environments.
4. Reduce the fear of the specific stimulus object or situation that previously provoked immediate anxiety so that there is little or no interference in normal routines.
5. Resolve panic symptoms and the fear that they will recur without an ability to cope with and control them.
6. Alleviate depressed mood and achieve a level of effective daily functioning.
7. Grieve losses in order to normalize mood.
8. Develop healthy cognitive patterns and beliefs about self and the world that lead to alleviation of anxiety, panic, or depressive symptoms.

___. _____

_____

___. _____

_____

___. _____

_____

SHORT-TERM OBJECTIVES	THERAPEUTIC INTERVENTIONS
1. Describe the nature of current symptoms and the symptom history of anxiety and depression. (1, 2)	1. Explore and assess the nature, severity, and history of the client's anxiety, panic, or depressive symptoms.
	2. Listen to the client's symptoms and express appropriate empathy for distressing feelings.
2. Cooperate with psychological testing to assess the severity of symptoms of anxiety and depression. (3)	3. Administer or refer the client for administration of psychological testing to assess for the presence and strength of anxiety or depression symptoms [e.g., Beck Depression Inventory (BDI), Mini Patient Health Survey, Minnesota Multiphasic Personality Inventory—2 (MMPI-2)].
3. Participate in an evaluation for suicidal ideation revealing current suicidal thoughts, plans, and access to means of suicide. (3, 4)	3. Administer or refer the client for administration of psychological testing to assess for the presence and strength of anxiety or depression symptoms (e.g., BDI, Mini Patient Health Survey, MMPI-2).
	4. Evaluate the client for suicidal thoughts, plans, or gestures. (See the Suicidal Ideation/Attempt chapter in the Offender and Victim Issues part of this Planner.)
4. Cooperate with an evaluation for hospitalization by identifying the extent of depressive symptoms and danger to self. (5)	5. Consider voluntary or involuntary hospitalization for the client by reviewing criteria for hospitalization with him/her, the hospital crisis worker, and the consulting psychiatrist.

5. Complete a thorough medical evaluation to assess for alternative causes for psychiatric symptoms and for the need for psychotropic medication. (6)

6. Take prescribed psychotropic medication as directed, reporting as to the medication's effectiveness and side effects. (7, 8)

7. Cooperate with a periodic reevaluation of symptomatology that uses psychological test instruments and/or interviews. (9, 10)

6. Refer the client for a complete physical evaluation in order to evaluate for a physiological basis for distressing symptoms (e.g., anemia, autoimmune disease such as chronic fatigue syndrome, nutritional deficiency) and a medication assessment.

7. Monitor the client for the effectiveness of and compliance with the prescribed psychotropic medication, encouraging him/her to take medication as directed.

8. Confer with the client's physician on a collaborative basis, discussing information regarding medication side effects, compliance, and effectiveness.

9. Administer psychological test inventories periodically to keep track of the client's symptoms.

10. Monitor the client's symptoms of depression, panic, and/or anxiety through pointed interview questioning regarding the frequency and depth of symptoms; validate his/her experience of symptoms by expressing empathy and reflective listening.

8. Verbalize an accurate description of the personal experiences of a panic attack and the phobic fear, disclosing fears that may appear to be unfounded or embarrassing. (11, 12)

9. Describe the posttraumatic stress disorder (PTSD) symptoms that cause distress and the actual trauma that triggers the associated memories and feelings. (13)

10. Identify negative self-talk and catastrophizing, which are associated with an increase in feelings of panic, anxiety, or depression. (14, 15)

11. Evaluate the client for panic attacks, helping him/her to describe in detail the symptoms that comprise a panic attack (e.g., dizziness, depersonalization, fear of dying or losing control) and the triggers for the symptoms.

12. Reassure the client that there is no connection between panic symptoms and heart attack, loss of behavioral control, or serious mental illness (i.e., "going crazy").

13. Evaluate the client for symptoms of PTSD, and apply cognitive behavioral techniques to decrease the symptoms. [See the Posttraumatic Stress Disorder (PTSD) chapter in the Victim Issues part of this Planner.]

14. Educate the client regarding the way thoughts influence feelings; assign him/her to read material on cognitive restructuring (e.g., *Mastery of Your Anxiety and Panic* by Barlow and Craske).

15. Help the client to identify his/her cognitions contributing to anxiety and depression (e.g., "I'm a failure"; "Things will never get any better"; "I'm inferior to ____ person").

11. Verbalize a connection between irrational beliefs and an increase in negative feelings. (16, 17)

12. Use verbal and written positive cues to build self-esteem and decrease symptoms. (18, 19)

13. Identify problem areas related to stressors, apply problem-solving techniques, and implement strategies to cope with stressors. (20, 21)

16. Assign the client to keep a daily log of level of anxiety or depression, daily events, and triggering thoughts that lead to a worsening of symptoms.

17. Using the client's journal material, assist him/her in identifying irrational beliefs that lead to depression and anxiety.

18. Assign the client to write out on a card a number of positive self-statements and to carry the list in his/her wallet or purse; ask him/her to look at the card three times per day and repeat positive self-statements silently.

19. Assign the client to read material on thought stopping (e.g., *The Relaxation and Stress Reduction Workbook* by Davis, Eshelman, and McKay); process this material and encourage implementation by him/her.

20. Teach the client a problem-solving process that includes brainstorming for alternative solutions, listing pros and cons of each option, implementing an action, and evaluating the outcome.

21. Construct a behavioral plan for the client to use in particularly stressful situations to decrease anxiety (e.g., leave situation and go to the restroom; take deep, slow breaths; review positive cue cards from purse or wallet, and repeat written positive affirmations).

14. Use daily exercise as a long-term anxiety reduction method. (22)

15. Use cognitive-behavioral techniques to reduce tension and stress. (23)

16. Use biofeedback training to improve ability to relax. (24)

17. Cooperate with a gradual desensitization procedure. (25, 26)

18. Identify behaviors that are self-defeating and may result in secondary gain. (27)

19. Identify and replace cognitions associated with low self-esteem. (28)

22. Encourage the client to exercise on a regular basis for overall anxiety reduction. (Recommend *Exercising Your Way to Better Mental Health* by Leith.)

23. Teach the client specific anxiety reduction techniques (e.g., meditation, deep breathing techniques, or positive guided imagery).

24. Administer to the client, or refer him/her for, biofeedback training to reduce his/her anxiety symptoms.

25. Assist the client in constructing a hierarchy of situations that increasingly evoke anxiety.

26. Use in vivo or imagined systematic desensitization techniques to gradually decrease the client's anxiety to a feared situation or phobic stimulus.

27. Alert the client to self-defeating behaviors that lead to increases in anxiety and depression (e.g., perfectionism, chronic self-criticism, pessimism, strong need for approval, codependency issues).

28. Evaluate the client for low self-esteem, and use cognitive strategies to improve dysfunctional thoughts. (See the Self-Esteem Deficits chapter in the Offender and Victim Issues part of this Planner.)

20. Cooperate with a periodic reevaluation of suicidal thoughts and feelings, reporting any increase of thoughts of harming self to the therapist immediately and participating in safety planning. (29, 30)

21. Verbalize a commitment to practice and improve coping skills on a long-term basis to prevent the recurrence of anxiety, depression, and panic symptoms. (31, 32, 33)

29. Continue reassessment of suicidal ideation and plan, evaluating for risk on a regular basis.

30. Develop a safety plan for the client to implement in case of recurrence of suicidal ideation (e.g., call someone in his/her support network, use the therapist's answering service, call the local crisis line and ask for help). (See the Suicidal Ideation/Attempt chapter in the Offender and Victim Issues part of this Planner.)

31. Help the client to identify long-term coping strategies [e.g., attending an assertiveness training class; committing to weekly attendance at a 12-step group, such as Codependents Anonymous (CoDA) or Survivors of Incest Anonymous (SIA); undertaking a long-term, six-month commitment to volunteer for a charity or cause that has personal importance) for depression and anxiety.

32. Develop a relapse plan in case depression or anxiety symptoms make a significant recurrence (e.g., medication reevaluation, consultation with the therapist, self-evaluation for triggers that have contributed to the exacerbation of symptoms).

33. Assist the client in writing a long-term self-care plan that includes exercise, improved nutrition, regular socialization, and renewed focus on appropriate vocational goals and spiritual needs.

__. _____   __. _____
    _____   _____

__. _____   __. _____
    _____   _____

__. _____   __. _____
    _____   _____

DIAGNOSTIC SUGGESTIONS:

ICD-9-CM	_ICD-10-CM_	_DSM-5_ Disorder, Condition, or Problem
300.02	F41.1	Generalized Anxiety Disorder
300.00	F41.9	Unspecified Anxiety Disorder
300.01	F41.0	Panic Disorder
300.22	F40.00	Agoraphobia
300.29	F40.xxx	Specific Phobia
309.24	F43.22	Adjustment Disorder, With Anxiety
309.0	F43.21	Adjustment Disorder, With Depressed Mood
296.xx	F31.xx	Bipolar I Disorder
296.89	F31.81	Bipolar II Disorder
300.4	F34.1	Persistent Depressive Disorder
301.13	F34.0	Cyclothymic Disorder
296.xx	F32.x	Major Depressive Disorder, Single Episode
296.xx	F33.x	Major Depressive Disorder, Recurrent Episode
295.70	F25.0	Schizoaffective Disorder, Bipolar Type
____	____	____
____	____	____

FAMILY REUNIFICATION*

BEHAVIORAL DEFINITIONS

1. Offender verbalizes a clear understanding of how abuse affected the victim, the family, and society, accepting full responsibility for the sexual offense.
2. Offender is truthful about his sexual history with an associated nondeceptive polygraph.
3. Offender agrees to a comprehensive therapeutic aftercare plan in order to assure the continuing safety of family members.
4. Offender has participated in a victim clarification process.
5. Nonoffending partner is able to verbalize ways in which the abuse has hurt not only the victim, but also siblings, extended family members, and society.
6. Nonoffending partner continues in own therapy for support.
7. Nonoffending partner has developed a family safety plan, which has a primary focus of protection of the children.
8. Nonoffending partner demonstrates a clear knowledge of the offender's relapse prevention plan and signs of sexual abuse.

---

*Family reunification in any form, ranging from written (letter) contact to the goal of reuniting the victim and the offender in the same residence, is a victim-focused process, with safety and support of the victim being the primary goal. Any professional participating in the reunification process should keep in mind that successful completion of a sex offender program does not eliminate the risk of reoffense. "Individuals who have sexually abused children will continue to present a risk to children even after successful treatment completion." (*Ethical Standards and Principles for the Management of Sexual Abusers* by the Association for the Treatment of Sexual Abusers, p. 32). Family reunification should be considered with a conservative impetus led by collaborating professionals with extensive training in victim treatment and sex offender evaluation and treatment, and clearly accepted by all parties that successful and safe reunification may not be possible.

9. All parties support reunification, including the victim, therapist for the victim, therapist for the spouse, therapist for the family, child protective services/social services, and the probation/parole officer.
10. Offender, nonoffending partner, and family agree to follow recommendations of the reunification team, consisting of therapists, social service agencies, and probation/parole officer.
11. The primary factor guiding the reunification process is safeguarding the victim, rather than maintaining the family no matter what the cost.

___. _____
_____
___. _____
_____
___. _____
_____

LONG-TERM GOALS

1. Nonoffending spouse makes an informed and free decision regarding reunification or separation in conjunction with the guidelines of the reunification team.
2. A safe reunification that meets the needs of the victim, other children, other family members, and the offender, and has a consensus of support from the respective therapists, agencies, and probation/parole officer.
3. All family members grieve the loss if nonreunification is the chosen direction.
4. Family promotes the safety and emotional well-being of the children.
5. Nuclear and extended family increase their support of the offender and his/her relapse prevention plan.

___. _____
_____
___. _____
_____
___. _____
_____

SHORT-TERM OBJECTIVES	THERAPEUTIC INTERVENTIONS
1. Verbalize an understanding of the reunification process and the factors that support or preclude reunification. (1)	1. Explain the process of possible reunification and the factors that influence such a decision (e.g., emotional stability of the family members, substance abuse, offender's abuse history and treatment compliance, victim's security, parenting skills, safety plan).
2. Comply with a psychosexual evaluation, a full-disclosure polygraph, and a sex offender treatment program. (2, 3, 4)	2. Refer the offender to an appropriately trained clinician for a thorough psychosexual evaluation, which is in accordance with the guidelines and standards of the Association for the Treatment of Sexual Abusers (ATSA).
	3. Require that the offender complete a full-disclosure polygraph with no evidence of deception.
	4. Evaluate the offender's competency to maintain an effective relapse prevention plan by interview and/or written assignments to determine whether he/she has successfully completed and meaningfully incorporated the concepts taught in a nondenial sex offender treatment program.
3. Family members comply with referrals for treatment and support. (5, 6, 7)	5. Assess the needs of the nonoffending partner, recommending attendance at a psychoeducational nonoffending partner group.

6. Evaluate family members and make a referral to the appropriate mental health professionals if behavioral, cognitive, or emotional problems are present.

7. Assess whether the offender clearly verbalizes full responsibility for the offense when he/she meets with the victim and other family members; assess and address any signs of retaliatory behavior toward the victim.

4. Verbalize full responsibility for the offense. (7)

7. Assess whether the offender clearly verbalizes full responsibility for the offense when he/she meets with the victim and other family members; assess and address any signs of retaliatory behavior toward the victim.

5. Family members, victim, and offender successfully complete the victim clarification process. (8)

8. Meet with the family to assess whether they have successfully completed the victim clarification process. (See *Just Before Dawn* by Hindman.)

6. Submit to an evaluation and guidance from the appropriate agencies. (9, 10)

9. Facilitate communication between members of a reunification team, which includes treatment providers, probation/parole officer, and child protective services; establish the common goal of victim safety.

10. Consult state sex offender treatment board, department of probation and parole, state sex offender monitoring program, or professional agencies [e.g., ATSA, California

7. Endorse the family safety plan that includes strategies to minimize the risk of reoffense and interventions, should the children be in danger. (11, 12)

8. Nonoffending partner verbalizes an understanding of relapse risks, signs of abuse, and the safety plan. (13, 14)

Professional Society on the Abuse of Children (CAP-SAC), or American Professional Society on the Abuse of Children (APSAC)] for guidelines to assist with the reunification process.

11. Review the offender's relapse prevention plan in the presence of all family members, and highlight all essential components (e.g., safety plan for the victim, supervision of the offender, role of probation/parole officer, ongoing treatment). (See *Connections Workbook* by Levinson and Morin.)

12. Teach both adults and children in the home how to identify the offender's behaviors that are associated with relapse (e.g., paying special attention to the victim, denial of the need for a safety plan, increased anger outbursts), and identify ways that they can protect themselves (e.g., informing the nonoffending partner of relapse behaviors observed, calling the probation officer or treatment providers).

13. Help the nonoffending partner to understand that the offender is at risk not only to repeat past offender patterns, but he/she may develop a new, inappropriate deviant sexual

focus (e.g., exhibitionism, child pornography, voyeurism). (See *Connections Workbook* by Levenson and Morin.)

14. Teach the nonoffending partner the signs of sexual abuse in children so he/she can remain on alert for any danger to the children; review a safety plan to be implemented if any suspicions of relapse arise. (See *Connections Workbook* by Levenson and Morin.)

9. Comply with supervision of contact with the victim as recommended by the reunification team. (15)

15. Adequately prepare for supervision of the offender, including placing on alert significant others, family, police, therapists, and victims. Train a designated supervisor in monitoring techniques and safety plan interventions.

10. Share family conflicts to reduce the impact of stressful events on recovery. (16)

16. Assist the family in managing crises unrelated to the sexual abuse (e.g., employment issues, financial problems, family illness, marital issues, military deployment), which will support the offender in his/her relapse prevention program.

11. Acknowledge that any further sexual abuse will result in permanent and immediate removal from the home and family contact. (17)

17. If sexual abuse recurs, contact proper agencies to remove the offender from the home immediately.

12. Accept family boundaries and the terms that all discipline of the children will be implemented by the nonoffending partner. (18)

13. Submit to a maintenance polygraph as ordered by probation/parole officer. (19)

14. Comply with ongoing monitoring, providing honest and complete information regarding maintaining the proper boundaries and each family member's emotional status. (20)

15. Consent to complete sex offender–specific treatment in accordance with ATSA guidelines. (21)

16. Victim verbalizes approval or disapproval of reunification plan. (22, 23, 24)

18. Teach the nonoffending partner principals of effective discipline, and address appropriate family boundaries (e.g., appropriate dress, bathroom rules, physical affection rules); emphasize that the offender does not discipline the children.

19. Require a periodic polygraph of the offender to evaluate that he/she is maintaining an offense-free lifestyle; coordinate this requirement with legal authorities as part of the probation/parole.

20. Continue monitoring and treatment until all victims and potential victims are 18 years old or emancipated from the home.

21. Assess whether the offender's treatment program is in accordance with ATSA guidelines regarding sex offender–specific treatment.

22. Review the treatment goals with the victim to make sure that he/she fully understands and is comfortable with the idea of reunification.

23. Encourage and monitor the victim's continuing involvement with his/her own treatment.

17. Nonoffending partner attend a psychoeducational course of treatment addressing issues related to keeping the family safe from sexual abuse. (25)

18. Accept a delay or termination of reunification if recommended by the reunification team. (26, 27)

24. Evaluate the benefit and risk to the victim and siblings if reunification of the offender with the family occurs.

25. Assign an educational program for the nonoffending partner that trains him/her in clues to look for regarding relapse, ways to support the victim, and precautions to take in protecting the victim and siblings. (See *Connections Workbook* by Levinson and Morin.)

26. Recommend a delay in reunification if the offender is in any denial of offense, shows consistently high levels of deviant arousal, or gives evidence of moderate to high reoffense risk in his/her psychosexual evaluation using risk assessment instruments and using polygraph, plethysmograph, and/or Abel Assessment for sexual interest. (See *Connections Workbook* by Levinson and Morin.)

27. Terminate or postpone the reunification process if significant prohibitory factors are discovered during an evaluation (e.g., offender psychopathy, multiple sex offenses, a polygraph indicating deception, current substance abuse, high levels of deviant arousal, reluctance from the victim, poor parenting skills on the part of the partner, emotional

19. Family members verbalize un-qualified support for the vic-tim. (28)

20. Family members agree to not keep secrets about sexual abuse, but to report suspicions or incidents. (29)

21. Victim expresses feelings of hurt and anger to the offender. (30)

22. Attend and participate in fam-ily therapy sessions addressing conflict resolution skills. (31)

instability in any family mem-ber, offender treatment non-compliance). (See *Connections Workbook* by Levenson and Morin.)

28. Within a family session, ad-dress the issue of divided loy-alties that family members may have in dealing with the victim and the offender; assure that the victim has adequate advocacy within the family.

29. With a family session, address the issue of *secrets,* distinguish-ing the difference between good secrets and bad secrets; teach that keeping abuse or suspicion of abuse a secret is destructive.

30. Within a family session, sup-port the victim as he/she faces the offender and directs appro-priate anger toward the of-fender because of the abuse while the offender empatheti-cally listens. (See *Just Before Dawn* by Hindman.)

31. Use role playing and modeling to teach the family conflict resolution skills (e.g., define the problem, propose a possi-ble solutions, evaluate pros and cons of each possible so-lution, select and implement an action that is mutually ac-ceptable, evaluate results) to deal with difficult issues that, in the past, have been buried (e.g., sexuality, anger, keeping secrets).

23. Comply with the recommendation against reunification, should this occur because of significantly dangerous risk factors, and process feelings. (27, 32, 33)

24. Family members attend multi-family group therapy. (34)

__. _____
   _____

__. _____
   _____

__. _____
   _____

27. Terminate or postpone the reunification process if significant prohibitory factors are discovered during an evaluation (e.g., offender psychopathy, multiple sex offenses, a polygraph indicating deception, current substance abuse, high levels of deviant arousal, reluctance from the victim, poor parenting skills on the part of the partner, emotional instability in any family member, offender treatment noncompliance). (See *Connections Workbook* by Levenson and Morin.)

32. Terminate the reunification and address related issues of grief and loss in family therapy sessions.

33. Maintain communication about the termination of reunification with the offender's probation officer, child protective services, and other team treatment providers.

34. Refer family members for multifamily group treatment that is focused on providing mutual support regarding sexual abuse experiences and reintegration challenges.

__. _____
   _____

__. _____
   _____

__. _____
   _____

DIAGNOSTIC SUGGESTIONS:

ICD-9-CM	_ICD-10-CM_	_DSM-5_ Disorder, Condition, or Problem
309.81	F43.10	Posttraumatic Stress Disorder
308.3	F43.0	Acute Stress Disorder
309.0	F43.21	Adjustment Disorder, With Depressed Mood
309.24	F43.22	Adjustment Disorder, With Anxiety
309.28	F43.23	Adjustment Disorder, With Mixed Anxiety and Depressed Mood
309.3	F43.24	Adjustment Disorder, With Disturbance of Conduct
309.4	F43.25	Adjustment Disorder, With Mixed Disturbance of Emotions and Conduct
312.9	F91.9	Unspecified Disruptive, Impulse Control, and Conduct Disorder
312.89	F91.8	Other Specified Disruptive, Impulse Control, and Conduct Disorder
313.81	F91.3	Oppositional Defiant Disorder
V61.22	Z69.011	Encounter for Mental Health Services for Perpetrator of Parental Child Abuse
V61.22	Z69.011	Encounter for Mental Health Services for Perpetrator of Parental Child Sexual Abuse
995.54	T74.12XA	Child Physical Abuse, Confirmed, Initial Encounter
995.54	T74.12XD	Child Physical Abuse, Confirmed, Subsequent Encounter
995.53	T74.22XA	Child Sexual Abuse, Confirmed, Initial Encounter
995.53	T74.22XD	Child Sexual Abuse, Confirmed, Subsequent Encounter
307.42	F51.01	Insomnia
300.6	F48.1	Depersonalization/Derealization Disorder
300.15	F44.9	Unspecified Dissociative Disorder
300.15	F44.89	Other Specified Dissociative Disorder
296.xx	F32.x	Major Depressive Disorder, Single Episode
296.xx	F33.x	Major Depressive Disorder, Recurrent Episode
301.7	F60.2	Antisocial Personality Disorder
301.83	F60.3	Borderline Personality Disorder
301.6	F60.7	Dependent Personality Disorder
————	————	————————————————
————	————	————————————————

SELF-ESTEEM DEFICIT

BEHAVIORAL DEFINITIONS

1. Feels unworthy of love and respect from others because of the sexual abuse/assault.
2. Sets inappropriately low life goals for self.
3. Makes self-disparaging remarks; sees self as unattractive, worthless, a loser, a burden, unimportant.
4. Takes blame easily.
5. Discounts or rejects compliments.
6. Difficulty saying no to others; assumes not being liked by others.
7. Fears rejection by others, especially peer group.
8. Uncomfortable in social situations, especially in larger groups.
9. Fails to maintain appropriate amount of eye contact.

—. _____
   _____
   _____
—. _____
   _____
   _____
—. _____
   _____

LONG-TERM GOALS

1. Develop a consistent, positive self-image.
2. Separate feelings about sexual trauma from value of self as a person.
3. Acknowledge self-value while condemning criminal acts.

—. _____
   _____

___. _____

   _____

___. _____

   _____

SHORT-TERM OBJECTIVES	THERAPEUTIC INTERVENTIONS
1. Acknowledge feelings of low self-value and low competence. (1, 2, 3)	1. Display unconditional positive regard toward the client, and encourage him/her to honestly verbalize thoughts and feelings about himself/herself.
	2. Verbalize empathy toward the client regarding his/her difficulty in acknowledging feelings of low self-esteem.
	3. Model respect toward the client.
2. Complete psychological inventories to assess self-esteem and identify areas for remediation. (4)	4. Administer psychological testing in order to assess the client's self-esteem (e.g., Rosenberg Self-Esteem Scale or Multidimensional Self-Esteem Inventory); evaluate the results and give feedback to him/her.
3. Identify childhood experiences that were destructive to self-esteem. (5, 6)	5. Assist the client in developing a family genogram to increase his/her awareness of family patterns of negative feedback and early messages regarding self-worth (e.g., harsh criticism as a child, extreme or unpredictable punishment, sexual abuse, abandonment, rejection, emotional isolation).

4. Identify feelings of being unlovable as a child and experiences that reinforced those feelings. (7)

5. Identify current experiences that have had a negative impact on self-esteem. (8)

6. Decrease the frequency of statements of low self-worth that stem from the external factors. (9)

7. Verbalize an increased awareness of how abuse/assault impacted self-esteem. (10)

8. Identify dysfunctional cognitions that are destructive to self-esteem. (11)

6. Explore the client's early relationship patterns and how he/she may still be striving to meet the unrealistic standards of key family members.

7. Explore the client's feelings of being unloved as a child, identifying the experiences that contributed to these negative feelings; help the client to focus responsibility for these experiences on the failures of caretakers, rather than himself/herself.

8. Explore the client's experiences that contribute to feelings of low self-esteem (e.g., sexual abuse, unusual physical features, criminal acts, severe poverty).

9. Teach the client that self-worth must be based on spiritual and/or intrinsic factors, not external circumstances.

10. Explore the impact of sexual abuse victimization or perpetration of sexual abuse/assault on the client's self-esteem and dysfunctional thoughts resulting from the abuse.

11. Challenge the client's dysfunctional thoughts that support his/her feelings of low self-esteem (e.g., blaming himself/herself when anything goes wrong in life, comparing himself/herself with others in a critical manner, maintaining standards of perfectionism, berating himself/herself for failures), and reinforce

thoughts that reflect movement toward positive self-regard.

9. Increase eye contact with others. (12)

12. Encourage increased eye contact by the client during the therapy session and during his/her interactions with others during daily life; reinforce progress noted.

10. Monitor daily cognitions and reaffirm positive aspects of self. (13)

13. Assign the client to keep a daily journal in order to increase his/her self-awareness; encourage him/her to attend more to positive thoughts and feelings regarding himself/herself.

11. Identify any secondary gain that results from speaking negatively about self and refusing to take any risks. (14)

14. Assist the client in identifying how self-disparagement and avoidance of risk taking could bring secondary gain (e.g., praise from others, others taking over responsibilities).

12. Increase the frequency of making positive statements about self. (15, 16, 17)

15. Assist the client in shifting his/her focus to the positive qualities of himself/herself when negative self-talk occurs in session.

16. Give the client positive feedback, and confront him/her when positive feedback is rejected or discounted.

17. Assign the client to make a list of his/her own assets and strengths.

13. Identify destructive, demeaning relationships, and replace these with positive, affirming relationships. (18, 19)

18. Assist the client in identifying relationships that are destructive to his/her self-esteem; explore ways to withdraw from these relationships.

14. Verbalize a commitment to respect self and to assertively expect respectful treatment from others.
(20, 21)

15. Respond to insults from others without self-deprecating cognitions.
(22, 23)

16. Verbalize strategies to positively cope with failures.
(24, 25)

19. Ask the client to commit to developing positive and supportive relationships as a life plan; assist him/her in identifying potential sources for support.

20. Teach the client assertiveness skills. (See the Anger Difficulties chapter in the Victim Issues part or the Anger Difficulties chapter in the Offender Issues part of this Planner.)

21. Encourage the client to assertively express his/her opinions to others and to take his/her own views and opinions seriously; teach him/her to respect himself/herself and expect respect from others.

22. Help the client to construct a visually vivid mental image to use as an effective counteraction to negative comments, insults, and so forth (e.g., a negative comment "bounces off of me").

23. Teach the client how to replace negative thinking about himself/herself with positive self-talk, using self-esteem-building exercises. (See *Ten Days to Self-Esteem!* by Burns.)

24. Help the client to counter negative thoughts that focus on past failures by using rational emotive therapy techniques (e.g., although I failed in my marriage, I am not a failure).

17. Attend appointments to address medical and dental needs, affirming self-worth. (26)

18. Verbalize an increased satisfaction with employment situation. (27, 28, 29, 30)

25. Reframe the client's experiences with failure as a necessary part of the learning process.

26. Encourage the client to follow through with medical care and dental care; monitor and reinforce progress.

27. Evaluate the client's vocational goals and current employment satisfaction; refer him/her for additional training or help him/her to make a plan to apply for a job that is more suited to his/her skills and experience.

28. Use modeling and role playing to teach the client different ways to ask for a raise.

29. Use modeling and role playing to teach the client assertive ways to disagree with a supervisor.

30. Process the client's feelings regarding authority figures, addressing current attitudes and linking them with feelings toward parents and figures in childhood.

19. Implement effective techniques for coping with stress. (31)

31. Assist the client in identifying appropriate stress management techniques. (See the Stress Management Deficits chapter in the Offender and Victim Issues part of this Planner.)

20. Demonstrate improved grooming habits, taking time for good hygiene and attractive dress. (32)

32. Assign the client to give daily attention to his/her grooming and hygiene; monitor and give feedback as necessary or warranted.

21. List concrete goals for the future. (33)

22. Engage in daily self-affirming activities. (34, 35)

33. Assist the client in constructing a list of goals for different areas of life and address steps to achieving aspirations.

34. Instruct the client regarding the use of positive affirmations, and teach other self-care techniques. (See *The Relaxation and Stress Reduction Workbook* by Davis, Eshelman, and McKay.)

35. Encourage the client to set aside time each day to learn about himself/herself, spending time in personal growth activities (e.g., reading inspirational materials, journal writing, and meditating).

___. _____
_____

___. _____
_____

___. _____
_____

___. _____
_____

___. _____
_____

___. _____
_____

DIAGNOSTIC SUGGESTIONS:

ICD-9-CM	_ICD-10-CM_	_DSM-5_ Disorder, Condition, or Problem
300.23	F40.10	Social Anxiety Disorder (Social Phobia)
300.4	F34.1	Persistent Depressive Disorder
296.xx	F32.x	Major Depressive Disorder, Single Episode
296.xx	F33.x	Major Depressive Disorder, Recurrent Episode
300.02	F41.1	Generalized Anxiety Disorder
300.00	F41.9	Unspecified Anxiety Disorder
309.81	F43.10	Posttraumatic Stress Disorder
_____	_____	_____
_____	_____	_____

SEXUAL DYSFUNCTION

BEHAVIORAL DEFINITIONS

1. Strong avoidance of and/or repulsion to any and all sexual contact in spite of a relationship of mutual caring and respect.
2. Recurrent lack of the usual physiological response of sexual excitement and arousal (i.e., genital lubrication and swelling, attaining and/or maintaining an erection).
3. Persistent delay in or absence of reaching orgasm after achieving arousal and in spite of sensitive sexual pleasuring by a caring partner.
4. Inhibited sexual desire manifesting itself as a consistent lack of subjective sense of enjoyment and pleasure during sexual activity.
5. Unexplainable feelings of anger, rage, or fear when coming into desired sexual contact with a partner.
6. Genital pain before, during, or after sexual intercourse.
7. Consistent or recurring involuntary spasm of the vagina that prohibits penetration for sexual intercourse.
8. Consistent participation in sexual activities on the Internet (cybersex), chat room affairs, masturbation while online, sexual video rooms, or pornography resulting in negative life.
9. Involvement in multiple intimate relationships at the same time.
10. Increase in fantasizing and masturbatory activities following interpersonal conflicts and negative affect.
11. Pattern of reenactment of sexual trauma and revictimization throughout life by choosing abusive partners.
12. Pervasive pattern of promiscuity or the sexualization of relationships.
13. Normal sexual activity triggers irrational fears, suppressed rage, low self-esteem, depression, or anxious insecurity since becoming a victim of sexual trauma.

14. Pattern of demeaning, emotionally or physically abusive sexual relationships that are hidden from others or from self through denial or dissociation.

—. _____

_____

—. _____

_____

—. _____

_____

LONG-TERM GOALS

1. Increase desire for and enjoyment of emotionally meaningful sexual activity within a relationship of mutual caring.
2. Attain and maintain physiological excitement response during sexual intercourse leading to orgasm or ejaculation, with a reasonable amount of time, intensity, and focus given to sexual stimulation.
3. Eliminate pain and experience subjective pleasure before, during, and after sexual intercourse.
4. Eliminate vaginal spasms that prohibit penile penetration during sexual intercourse, and achieve a sense of relaxed enjoyment of coital pleasure.
5. Decrease inappropriate sexualization of relationships and increase the capacity for healthy, meaningful intimacy.
6. Reduce the impact of childhood sexual abuse or later-life sexual trauma on current sexuality, with resultant enjoyment of appropriate, respectful sexual contact.
7. Heed appropriate physical boundaries, engaging in sexual behavior only when it is respectful, mutually desired, and based in a loving relationship.

—. _____

_____

—. _____

_____

—. _____

_____

SHORT-TERM OBJECTIVES

1. Explore feelings and beliefs about sex, identifying specific problem areas. (1, 2)

2. Identify family attitudes about sexuality and own early childhood experiences regarding relationships and sexuality. (3, 4)

3. Verbalize the ways that own early religious/moral upbringing has impacted life, and link to current sexual attitudes, behaviors, and feelings. (5)

4. Verbalize an increased understanding of intimacy. (6)

THERAPEUTIC INTERVENTIONS

1. Direct the client to openly describe sexual difficulties, preoccupations, or repulsions, including any pain or discomfort associated with sexual activities.

2. Empathically acknowledge the client's discomfort with or resistance to discussing sexuality.

3. Explore the client's history of sexual development, including social successes and failures in adolescence, peer relationships, and romantic relationships; assign the completion of a sexual autobiography, including any episodes of abuse/assault.

4. Explore the client's early family messages about sexuality, examining negative messages or abusive experiences from his/her family of origin.

5. Explore the nature and extent that the client's religious training and moral prohibitions have had on forming attitudes about sexuality and how these influence current feelings and sexual practices.

6. Assist the client in defining a healthy sexual relationship, reviewing qualities of intimate human relationships (e.g., emotional closeness, reciprocity, trust) and assigning him/her to list 10 aspects of intimacy.

5. Verbalize a greater understanding of human sexuality and misconceptions. (7, 8)

7. Assign the client to attend a sex education class to address issues related to sexuality (e.g., risk of sexually transmitted diseases, responsibility of informing a partner about own sexually transmitted disease, sexual myths).

8. Recommend that the client read material on human sexuality to increase his/her understanding and to correct misconceptions. (See *Sex for Dummies* by Westheimer, *Becoming Orgasmic: A Sexual Growth Program for Women* by Heiman and LoPiccolo, *Sexual Awareness* by McCarthy and McCarthy, or *The Gift of Sex* by Penner and Penner.)

6. Define the boundaries of appropriate physical touching in various social contexts. (9)

9. Assist the client in defining appropriate touch (e.g., shaking hands at a social introduction, giving a high five, greeting a friend with a hug, or directing someone by touching an elbow), noting how appropriate touching may vary in different settings (e.g., correctional setting, funeral, family function).

7. Verbalize an understanding of how harmful it can be to become obsessed with cybersex, chat room affairs, pornography, 900-number sex lines, or multiple sex partners. (10)

10. Assist the client in understanding how promiscuity, pornography preoccupation, and cybersex obsession are related to loneliness, unresolved emotional conflicts, impersonalization, and avoidance of real intimacy.

8. Acknowledge the negative impact of sexual abuse trauma on current sexual attitudes and behavior. (11, 12)

9. Partner verbalize an understanding of how sexual abuse has had a negative impact on the client's sexuality. (13)

10. Identify negative self-talk that triggers sexual discomfort, and replace it with positive healthy thoughts that improve sexual attitudes. (14)

11. Describe the amount and frequency of any drug that is ingested, including prescription medication and alcohol. (15, 16)

12. Complete a thorough medical examination to rule out possible organic causes for sexual dysfunction. (17, 18)

11. Explore the client's sexual trauma–related memories (e.g., postrape exam, childhood sexual abuse, history of sexual violence) and the emotional impact on current sexual attitudes and behavior.

12. Assist the client in linking his/her compulsive masturbation, multiple partners, sexual aversion, or lack of emotional gratification in sexual relations to the negative effects of his/her sexual abuse trauma.

13. Facilitate a conjoint session with the client and his/her partner, and evaluate the partner's response to their sexual problems related to the client's history of sexual trauma; assign the couple to read together material on the negative sexual effect of sexual abuse. (See *The Survivor's Guide to Sex* by Haines.)

14. Assist the client in identifying his/her negative self-talk that triggers sexual aversion; replace it with positive cognitive messages.

15. Review the client's current medications (e.g., antidepressants, antihypertensives, anticonvulsants) that may affect sexual desire or functioning.

16. Evaluate the client for alcohol or other substance abuse that may affect sexual functioning.

17. Refer the client to a physician for a complete physical to evaluate the possible physiological or organic origin of low or no sexual desire.

13. Identify and resolve negative feelings that are related to or that may impede sexual functioning in relationships. (19, 20)

14. Practice sensate focus exercises alone and with partner, and share feelings associated with this activity. (21, 22)

18. Teach the client how physiological conditions (e.g., low testosterone levels, diabetes, menopause) can impact sexuality and how medical treatment from a physician can remediate symptoms.

19. Encourage the client to disclose his/her feelings of guilt, shame, depression, and anxiety related to sexual history, relationship issues, and current life status; assess how these feelings affect his/her sexual functioning.

20. Focus therapy on resolution of negative emotions that are affecting current sexual functioning. (See the Self-Blame or Trust Impairment chapters in the Victim Issues part, or the Anxiety, Panic, and Depression chapter in the Offender and Victim Issues part of this Planner.)

21. Assign the client to practice with his/her partner graduated steps of sexual pleasuring exercises that reduce performance anxiety and focus on experiencing bodily arousal sensations. (See *When a Woman's Body Says No to Sex* by Valins or *Becoming Orgasmic: A Sexual Growth Program for Women* by Heiman and LoPiccolo.)

15. Identify the antecedents and consequences of infidelity. (23, 24, 25)

16. List the negative effects of unconventional sex practices. (26)

22. Assign reading materials (e.g., *Inhibited Sexual Desire* by Knopf and Seiler, *The New Joy of Sex* by Comfort, *Sex Over 50* by Block) that provide accurate sexual and relationship information, along with outlining sexual exercises that disinhibit and reinforce sexual sensate focus.

23. Encourage the client to explore and clarify feelings and issues that contribute to and result from infidelity (e.g., difficulties/fears with intimacy, relationship problems, hostility toward the partner, lack of respect for the partner).

24. Assign the client to read material on the impact of an affair on a relationship (e.g., *After the Affair* by Abrahms-Spring or *Surviving Infidelity* by Subotnik and Harris); process key concepts that were learned.

25. Discuss the consequences to the client and his/her partner that result from unfaithfulness.

26. Assist the client in seeing that chaotic sexual practices (e.g., three-way sex, attending sadomasochistic sex clubs) destabilize relationships, create insecurity in the partner, communicate that the partner is inadequate, and demean sexual intimacy.

17. Identify gender confusion issues that may be affecting sexual behavior. (27)

18. Verbally identify the specific behaviors, attitudes, and feelings that lead to compulsive sexual behaviors and the consequences to self and partner. (28, 29)

19. Describe the nature and frequency of the use of the Internet for sexual gratification. (30)

20. Identify the negative effects of cybersex. (31, 32, 33)

27. Explore sexual orientation issues, including homosexual interests and anxieties, and gender identity confusion that may influence heterosexual anxiety or disinterest.

28. Probe the client's sexual practices for the compulsive use of sex as a way to avoid feelings; explore for problems that the pressure for frequent sexual gratification has caused in his/her life.

29. Assign the client to read material on sexual compulsion (e.g., *Out of the Shadows: Understanding Sexual Addiction* by Carnes, *Don't Call It Love: Recovery from Sexual Addiction* by Carnes, or *Sexual Anorexia* by Carnes); discuss key concepts that he/she has learned.

30. Explore the client's use of the Internet for sexual arousal and gratification, noting frequency of use, and depth of pathology of his/her cybersexual behavior.

31. Discuss the realistic aspects of Internet-based sexual contact (e.g., not real relationships, based on fantasy, promote pseudointimacy).

32. Teach the client how cybersex behavior can contribute to marital problems, affairs, and incest fantasies.

33. Assign readings and written exercises in the workbook *Cybersex Unhooked* (Delmonico, Griffin, and Moriarity), and process in session.

21. Attend a 12-step group that focuses on overcoming sexual dependency or addiction. (34)

34. Refer the client to a 12-step group for prevention of relapse and emotional support (e.g., Sexual Addicts Anonymous, Sexaholics Anonymous, Sex and Love Addictions Anonymous).

22. Identify fears and misconceptions about intimacy in relationships. (35, 36, 37)

35. Discuss how the client has viewed sex as the only way to become intimate with someone, or as a sign that someone loved or wanted you; trace how this developed into a sexual obsession.

36. Explore the client's fears about building intimacy with his/her current partner or potential partner.

37. Discuss how increased preoccupation with sexual fantasy may function as a substitute for emotional intimacy because of fear of rejection.

23. List the tools to use when the urge to relapse recurs, and express confidence in their effectiveness and own ability to be in control. (38)

38. Help the client to develop coping strategies (e.g., attend sexual addiction 12-step group, call a support person on the phone, spiritual focus) to deal with negative emotional states as alternatives to sexually compulsive/addictive behaviors.

24. Verbalize ethical and moral principles to live by and articulate a lifelong plan for managing addictive tendencies. (39)

39. Reinforce the verbalization of a lifelong plan of risk reduction and promotion of healthy sexual behaviors in an intimate relationship.

__. _____   __. _____
     _____   _____

__. _____   __. _____
     _____   _____

__. _____   __. _____
     _____   _____

DIAGNOSTIC SUGGESTIONS:

ICD-9-CM	_ICD-10-CM_	_DSM-5_ Disorder, Condition, or Problem
302.71	F52.22	Female Sexual Interest/Arousal Disorder
302.79	F52.0	Male Hypoactive Sexual Desire
302.73	F52.31	Female Orgasmic Disorder
302.76	F52.6	Genito-Pelvic Pain/Penetration Disorder
302.9	F52.9	Unspecified Sexual Dysfunction
302.72	F52.21	Erectile Disorder
302.75	F52.4	Premature Ejaculation
302.74	F52.32	Delayed Ejaculation
302.85	F64.1	Gender Dysphoria in Adolescents and Adults

_____ _____ _____

_____ _____ _____

STRESS MANAGEMENT DEFICITS

BEHAVIORAL DEFINITIONS

1. Engages in dysfunctional behaviors (e.g., alcohol abuse, social withdrawal, overspending, impulsive sex) in response to stress.
2. Feelings of being overwhelmed by stressors.
3. Increase in psychosomatic symptoms (i.e., vague physical symptoms that have no organic foundation) when faced with stress.
4. Worsening of stress-related illnesses (e.g., asthma, migraine headaches, ulcers, hypertension) due to psychosocial stressors.
5. Feelings of anxiety and depression secondary to stressors in life.
6. Lack of self-care in the areas of hygiene, appearance, health-related activities, exercise, sleep, nutrition, spirituality, and social interactions.

__. _____
   _____
__. _____
   _____
__. _____
   _____

LONG-TERM GOALS

1. Improved stress management skills, resulting in reduced emotional and physical consequences of stress.
2. Ability to generate multiple solutions to current and future problems, and implement a problem-solving plan.
3. Increased interactions with social support system of family and friends.

4. Devote adequate attention and time to daily self-care.
5. Increased assertiveness by exercising own rights while respecting the rights of others.

__. _____

_____

__. _____

_____

__. _____

_____

SHORT-TERM OBJECTIVES

THERAPEUTIC INTERVENTIONS

1. Identify the stressors that are experienced in current life. (1, 2)

1. Assist the client in identifying stressors in his/her life and the impact that they have on physical and emotional functioning.

2. Administer the Schedule of Recent Experience to elicit information about life events and the client's emotional response to them.

2. Differentiate the types of stressors present and the intensity of the emotional reaction to them, including general life events, daily hassles, and chronically difficult life situations. (3, 4)

3. Assign the client to keep a daily journal of stressors, degree of emotional reaction, and behavioral coping responses.

4. Help the client to differentiate the types of stressors in his/her life (e.g., interpersonal conflicts, vocational or financial issues, parenting concerns, personal expectations); rate the relative intensity of his/her emotional reactions to these events.

3. Identify the self-destructive coping behaviors used to respond to stressors. (5, 6)

4. Read material that is informative regarding coping with stressors to gain knowledge about how other people cope. (7)

5. Implement breathing and relaxation techniques at least three times daily to decrease tension. (8, 9, 10, 11)

5. Assist the client in identifying the dysfunctional, self-destructive, self-defeating coping behaviors that have been implemented in response to stress (e.g., alcohol abuse, social withdrawal, overspending, impulsive sex).

6. Assign the client to list the negative consequences that have occurred due to his/her implementing self-destructive coping mechanisms.

7. Assign the client to read material relevant to stress reduction. (See *The Book of Stress Survival: Identifying and Reducing the Stress in Your Life* by Kirsta or *The Relaxation and Stress Reduction Workbook* by Davis, Eshelman, and McKay.)

8. Teach the client to become more aware of his/her breathing patterns and to shift to deep, rhythmic, abdominal breathing as a way of calming himself/herself.

9. Teach the client effective relaxation skills (e.g., structured deep muscle relaxation exercises, self-hypnosis, autogenics).

10. Seek a commitment from the client to incorporate relaxation techniques that reduce stress in his/her daily routine.

6. Identify negative self-talk that leads to increased anxiety, decreased self-esteem, hopelessness, and overall poor emotional functioning. (12, 13)

7. Verbalize the advantage of using positive self-talk. (14)

8. Implement positive self-talk to increase confidence and reduce anxiety. (15, 16)

11. Help the client to problem-solve to remove impediments to implementing a daily relaxation plan.

12. Teach the client how internal dialogue and mental imagery can lead to negative affect and maladaptive behavior.

13. Assist the client in identifying his/her distorted, negative cognitions that lead to decreased self-esteem, lack of confidence, pessimism, and self-destructive coping responses to stressors.

14. Ask the client to develop and process a list of how thinking positively about himself/herself could improve his/her quality of life (e.g., decrease thoughts of hopelessness, leading to increased self-confidence; reduce depression and anxiety, resulting in improved mood; increase positive self-image, leading to increased socialization).

15. Ask the client to make a list of positive self-talk and mental images about himself/herself and the future that improve self-esteem, encourage confidence, and support a positive view of the future.

16. Assign the client to engage in positive self-talk at least three times per day and especially at times of increased stress.

9. Verbalize being able to see self as challenged, rather than threatened, by stress. (17)

10. List and implement the steps of the problem-solving process. (18, 19)

11. Apply problem-solving techniques to three stressors, and discuss the effectiveness of the strategies. (20)

12. Identify situations where social anxiety impedes having needs met. (21, 22)

17. Assist the client in developing a more positive attitude regarding coping skills by modeling positive verbalizations that can be used in response to stressors.

18. Teach the client the steps in effective problem solving (e.g., problem clarification, brainstorming, evaluation of options, implementation, and outcome assessment).

19. Assign the client to keep a journal of the process of problem-solving of a current stressor by clearly defining the problem, brainstorming, and then evaluating possible solutions, implementing chosen options, and assessing the outcome; process the journal material with him/her.

20. Assist the client in applying new problem-solving skills to address three current stressors; process the results of implementation.

21. Administer the Leibowitz Social Anxiety Scale or the Social Phobia Inventory to the client, and discuss areas of social discomfort with him/her.

22. Assist the client in identifying his/her distorted cognitions associated with anxiety-producing social situations.

13. Initiate new social contacts, and cope with uncomfortable social anxiety using positive self-talk and thought-stopping techniques. (23)

14. Make a commitment to practice assertive behavior daily, and keep a log of the experience. (24, 25)

15. Develop and verbalize a plan for constructive action to reduce vocational stress. (26)

16. Present a written plan for appropriately balancing time spent on various prioritized daily activities. (27, 28)

23. Teach the client social anxiety coping behaviors through the use of modeling and role play of positive self-talk and thought-stopping in interactions with others.

24. Using modeling, role playing, and behavior rehearsal, teach the client how to use the assertive formula, "I feel . . . when you. . . . I would prefer it if. . . ." in difficult situations.

25. Assign the client to initiate one new assertive behavior daily, identify negative self-talk, and replace the distorted cognitions with positive thoughts about himself/herself; ask him/her to record these experiences in a journal, and process the material.

26. Assist the client in developing a proactive plan for addressing his/her vocational stress issues (e.g., decreasing conflicts with coworkers and supervisors, realistic appraisal of his/her employment strengths and weaknesses, vocational goals, training needs).

27. Teach the client how time management strategies can contribute to a balanced life so that he/she can achieve more and feel less daily pressure and tension.

28. Assign the client to prioritize his/her time allotment to various activities through the day and week using time management strategies.

17. Identify positive rewards that are associated with an increase in self-care behaviors and a decrease in harmful behaviors. (29, 30)

29. Assign the client to keep a journal tracking unhealthy behaviors (e.g., consumption of alcohol, smoking, eating habits, and sleeping habits) for one week.

30. Teach the client the benefits of an individual positive self-care plan, and assign him/her to list the long-term positive and negative impact of behaviors in his/her current lifestyle (e.g., sleep habits, exercise pattern, medical and dental care habits, eating style, alcohol and tobacco use, hours spent at work).

18. Make a long-term commitment to change unhealthy lifestyle to one of balanced activities that promote a positive sense of well-being and optimal physical and emotional health. (31)

31. Assist the client in developing a balanced lifestyle (e.g., work, play, nutrition, exercise, sleep, quiet time, relationships); encourage him/her to follow through with implementing the plan.

__. _____
   _____
__. _____
   _____
__. _____
   _____

__. _____
   _____
__. _____
   _____
__. _____
   _____

DIAGNOSTIC SUGGESTIONS:

ICD-9-CM	_ICD-10-CM_	_DSM-5_ Disorder, Condition, or Problem
309.0	F43.21	Adjustment Disorder, With Depressed Mood
308.3	F43.0	Acute Stress Disorder
300.81	F45.1	Somatic Symptom Disorder
300.23	F40.10	Social Anxiety Disorder (Social Phobia)
300.4	F34.1	Persistent Depressive Disorder
296.xx	F32.x	Major Depressive Disorder, Single Episode
296.xx	F33.x	Major Depressive Disorder, Recurrent Episode
300.02	F41.1	Generalized Anxiety Disorder
_____	_____	_____
_____	_____	_____

SUBSTANCE ABUSE

BEHAVIORAL DEFINITIONS

1. To escape from feelings of shame, depression, and anger related to being a victim of sexual abuse, consistent use of alcohol or other mood-altering drugs until high, intoxicated, or passed out.
2. To escape from feelings of guilt related to committing a sexual offense, consistent use of alcohol or other mood-altering drugs until high, intoxicated, or passed out.
3. Inability to stop or cut down use of a mood-altering drug once started, despite the verbalized desire to do so and the negative consequences that continued use brings.
4. Blood work that reflects the results of a pattern of heavy substance use (elevated liver enzymes).
5. Denial that chemical dependence is a problem, despite direct feedback from spouse, relatives, friends, and employers that the use of the substance is negatively affecting them and others.
6. Amnestic blackouts have occurred when abusing alcohol.
7. Continued drug and/or alcohol use, despite experiencing persistent or recurring physical, legal, vocational, social, or relationship problems that are directly caused by the use of the substance.
8. Increased tolerance for the mood-altering drug, as there is the need to use more to become intoxicated or to attain the desired effect.
9. Physical symptoms (e.g., shaking, seizures, nausea, headaches, sweating, anxiety, insomnia, and/or depression) when withdrawing from the substance.
10. Suspension of important social, recreational, or occupational activities because they interfere with substance abuse.
11. Large time investment in activities to obtain the substance, to use it, or to recover from its effects.
12. Consumption of the substance in greater amounts and for longer periods than intended.

13. Continued use of the mood-altering chemical after being told by a physician that it is causing health problems.
14. Relapse into abuse of mood-altering substances after a substantial period of sobriety.

___. _____

_____

___. _____

_____

___. _____

_____

LONG-TERM GOALS

1. Resolve emotional conflicts that contribute to using substance abuse as an attempt to escape.
2. Accept chemical dependence, and begin to actively participate in a recovery program.
3. Establish a sustained recovery, free from the use of all mood-altering substances.
4. Acquire the necessary skills to establish and maintain long-term sobriety from all mood-altering chemicals.
5. Withdraw from mood-altering substance, stabilize physically and emotionally, and then establish a supportive recovery plan.
6. Develop an awareness of a personal pattern of relapse, physical relapse triggers, and the coping strategies needed to deal with them effectively.

___. _____

_____

___. _____

_____

___. _____

_____

SHORT-TERM OBJECTIVES

1. Describe the amount, frequency, and history of substance abuse. (1, 2)

2. Identify the negative consequences of drug and/or alcohol abuse. (3, 4)

3. Obtain a medical examination to evaluate the effects of chemical dependence. (5)

4. Make verbal "I" statements that reflect acknowledgment and acceptance of chemical dependence. (6, 7)

THERAPEUTIC INTERVENTIONS

1. Gather a complete drug and/or alcohol history, including amount and pattern of use, signs and symptoms of use, and negative life consequences (e.g., social, legal, medical, familial, and vocational) resulting from the client's chemical dependence.

2. Administer the Alcohol Severity Index, and process the results with the client.

3. Ask the client to make a list of the ways that substance abuse has negatively impacted his/her life; process this list, and assist him/her in adding consequences that have been overlooked.

4. Assign the client to ask two or three people who are close to him/her to write a letter to the therapist in which they identify how they saw his/her chemical dependence negatively impacting his/her life.

5. Refer the client for a thorough physical examination to determine any negative medical effects of chemical dependence.

6. Assign the client to complete a first-step paper and to process it with either the group, sponsor, or therapist to receive feedback.

7. Require the client to attend didactic lectures related to chemical dependence and the process of recovery. Then ask him/her to identify in writing several key points attained from each lecture for further processing with the therapist.

5. Decrease the level of denial around use as evidenced by fewer statements about minimizing the amount of use and its negative impact on life. (3, 8)

3. Ask the client to make a list of the ways that substance abuse has negatively impacted his/her life; process this list, and assist him/her in adding consequences that have been overlooked.

8. Model and reinforce statements that reflect acceptance of chemical dependence and its destructive consequences for the client and others.

6. Verbalize increased knowledge of alcoholism and the process of recovery. (7, 9)

7. Require the client to attend didactic lectures related to chemical dependence and the process of recovery. Then ask him/her to identify in writing several key points attained from each lecture for further processing with the therapist.

9. Assign the client to read an article or pamphlet or the *AA Big Book* [Alcoholics Anonymous (AA)] on the disease concept of alcoholism and select several key ideas to discuss with the therapist.

7. Verbalize an understanding of emotional, social, and family factors that foster chemical dependence. (10, 11)

8. Describe childhood experience of alcohol abuse by immediate and extended family members. (12)

9. Review extended family alcohol and drug use history and related patterns of sexual abuse and sexual trauma within the family history. (13)

10. Identify the ways that being sober could positively impact life. (14)

11. Identify changes that need to be made in personal life that will support sobriety. (15)

12. State changes that will be made in social relationships to support recovery. (16)

10. Assess the client's intellectual, emotional, and cognitive functioning regarding their contribution to chemical dependence; focus on the underlying emotional conflict that may contribute to escapism.

11. Investigate situational stress factors that may foster the client's chemical dependence, including abuse and trauma issues.

12. Probe the client's family history for chemical dependence patterns, and relate these to his/her use.

13. Explore extended family chemical dependence history, and relate this to patterns of sexual abuse and sexual assault within family.

14. Ask the client to make and process a list of how being sober could positively impact his/her life.

15. Assist the client in developing an insight into life changes (e.g., living situation, friendships, recreational activities, employment) that may be needed in order to maintain long-term sobriety.

16. Review the negative influence of continuing current alcohol- or drug-related friendships, and assist the client in making a plan to develop new friendships.

13. List recreational and social activities (and places) that will replace substance abuse–related activities. (17)

14. Identify constructive proj-ects that will be accomplished now that time and energy are available in sobriety. (18)

15. Agree to make amends to significant others who have been hurt by the life dominated by substance abuse. (19)

16. Identify the positive impact that sobriety will have on intimate and family relationships. (20)

17. Verbalize how the living situation contributes to chemical dependence and acts as a hindrance to recovery. (21, 22)

18. Develop a plan for a more stable, healthy living situation that will support recovery. (23)

19. Terminate the current living situation, and move to a place that is more conducive to recovery. (24)

17. Assist the client in planning social and recreational activities that are free from association with substance abuse.

18. Plan household or work-related projects that can be accomplished to build self-esteem now that sobriety affords time and energy for such constructive activity.

19. Discuss the negative effects that substance abuse has had on family, friends, and work relationships, and encourage a plan to make amends for such hurt.

20. Assist the client in identifying positive changes in family relationships that can result from recovery.

21. Evaluate the role of the client's living situation in fostering a pattern of chemical dependence.

22. Assign the client to write a list of negative influences for chemical dependence inherent in his/her current living situation.

23. Encourage and assist the client in developing a plan for a change in his/her living situation that will foster recovery.

24. Reinforce positive changes in the client's living situation.

20. Write a good-bye letter to the drug of choice telling it why it must go. (25)

21. Sign an abstinence contract and verbalize feelings of fear, grief, or reluctance associated with signing it. (26)

22. Develop a written aftercare plan that will support the maintenance of long-term sobriety. (16, 17, 27, 28)

23. Attend AA/NA meetings on a regular basis as frequently as necessary to support sobriety. (28)

24. Identify sources of ongoing support in maintaining sobriety. (29)

25. Direct the client to write a good-bye letter to the drug of choice; read it and process related feelings.

26. Develop an abstinence contract with the client regarding the use of his/her drug of choice; process the emotional impact of this contract.

16. Review the negative influence of continuing current alcohol- or drug-related friendships, and assist the client in making a plan to develop new friendships.

17. Assist the client in planning social and recreational activities that are free from association with substance abuse.

27. Assign and review the client's written aftercare plan to ensure that it is adequate to maintain sobriety.

28. Recommend that the client attend AA or Narcotics Anonymous (NA) meetings, and report the impact of the meetings in future sessions.

28. Recommend that the client attend AA or NA meetings, and report the impact of the meetings in future sessions.

29. Explore the client's positive support system available in sobriety, and discuss ways to develop and reinforce a positive support system.

25. Meet with an Alcoholics Anonymous/Narcotics Anonymous (AA/NA) member to gain information about the role of AA/NA in recovery. (30)

26. Identify potential relapse triggers, and develop strategies for constructively dealing with each trigger. (31, 32)

27. Describe the sexual issues that play a role in triggering substance abuse or relapse. (33)

28. Develop a written aftercare plan with a focus on coping with sexual issues, sexual trauma, and uncomfortable feelings related to sexual difficulties. (34)

30. Assign the client to meet with an AA/NA member who has been working the 12-step program for several years, and find out specifically how the program has helped him/her stay sober; process this meeting.

31. Help the client to develop an awareness of relapse triggers (e.g., emotional conflicts, situational factors, social issues) and alternative ways of handling them effectively.

32. Recommend that the client read *Staying Sober: A Guide to Relapse Prevention* (Gorski and Miller) and *The Staying Sober Workbook* (Gorski).

33. Assist the client in identifying sexual issues related to relapse.

34. Assign the client to develop and process an aftercare plan that addresses relapse triggers that are related to sexual abuse/trauma.

__. _____
   _____
__. _____
   _____
__. _____
   _____

DIAGNOSTIC SUGGESTIONS:

ICD-9-CM	_ICD-10-CM_	_DSM-5_ Disorder, Condition, or Problem
303.90	F10.20	Alcohol Use Disorder, Moderate or Severe
305.00	F10.10	Alcohol Use Disorder, Mild
304.30	F12.20	Cannabis Use Disorder, Moderate or Severe
305.20	F12.10	Cannabis Use Disorder, Mild
304.20	F14.20	Cocaine Use Disorder, Moderate or Severe
305.60	F14.10	Cocaine Use Disorder, Mild
305.70	F15.10	Amphetamine Use Disorder, Mild
304.40	F15.20	Amphetamine Use Disorder, Moderate or Severe
305.50	F11.10	Opioid Use Disorder, Mild
304.00	F11.20	Opioid Use Disorder, Moderate or Severe
305.90	F18.10	Inhalant Use Disorder, Mild
304.60	F18.20	Inhalant Use Disorder, Moderate or Severe
291.2	F10.27	Moderate or Severe Alcohol Use Disorder With Alcohol-Induced Major Neurocognitive Disorder, Nonamnestic-Confabulatory Type
291.1	F10.26	Moderate or Severe Alcohol Use Disorder With Alcohol-Induced Major Neurocognitive Disorder, Amnestic-Confabulatory Type
V71.01	Z72.811	Adult Antisocial Behavior
300.4	F34.1	Persistent Depressive Disorder
312.34	F63.81	Intermittent Explosive Disorder
309.81	F43.10	Posttraumatic Stress Disorder
304.10	F13.20	Sedative, Hypnotic, or Anxiolytic Use Disorder, Moderate or Severe
301.7	F60.2	Antisocial Personality Disorder

SUICIDAL IDEATION/ATTEMPT

BEHAVIORAL DEFINITIONS

1. Verbalizations expressing that suicide is a reasonable choice in an emotionally difficult situation.
2. Has issued a direct verbal warning that there will be an attempt to end life.
3. Has made a specific, detailed, lethal, and viable plan for suicide.
4. The intent to commit suicide is communicated indirectly by actions (e.g., writing a will, making gifts of important possessions, purchasing a weapon).
5. Depression associated with risk factors (e.g., hopelessness, social isolation, recent grief, prior suicide attempts, history of impulsivity, substance abuse, history of sexual abuse, caught in a shameful act).
6. Overwhelmed by feelings of guilt and shame related to being a victim of sexual abuse.
7. Feelings of shame and guilt regarding sex abuse perpetration being brought to light.
8. A dramatic and sudden improvement in serious depressive affect without any significant improvement in environmental conditions or emotional skills.
9. A recent suicide attempt.
10. Positive family history of depression, suicide, or preoccupation with suicidal thoughts/attempts.

___. _____
_____
___. _____
_____
___. _____
_____

LONG-TERM GOALS

1. Identify and resolve emotional conflicts that have led to hopelessness and suicidal urges.
2. Use cognitive behavioral treatment to address and challenge faulty cognitions that lead to an increase in suicidal ideation.
3. Stabilize the crisis by using hospitalization.
4. Improve problem-solving skills.
5. Develop strategies to increase tolerance for stress.
6. Alleviate suicidal impulses, and reestablish a sense of hope for self and the future.

__. _____
   _____
__. _____
   _____
__. _____
   _____

SHORT-TERM OBJECTIVES

1. Participate in an evaluation of suicidal ideation revealing current suicidal thoughts, plans, and access to means, as well as general mood variability, any thought disorder, or impulse control issues. (1, 2)

THERAPEUTIC INTERVENTIONS

1. Conduct a thorough and comprehensive assessment of the history, frequency, content, and intensity of the client's suicidal ideation.

2. Diagnose the underlying psychopathology, paying particular attention to those diagnostic categories that may be associated with a higher vulnerability to suicidal risk (e.g., major depression, bipolar disorder, schizophrenia, posttraumatic stress disorder, borderline or antisocial personality disorder).

2. Disclose traumatic life events, including physical, emotional, and sexual abuse. (3)

3. Explore the client's suicide risk factors, especially a history of childhood sexual and physical abuse.

3. Describe the details of prior history of suicide attempts. (4, 5, 6)

4. Ask the client to sign a form for authorization to release information to request and review his/her medical records, particularly those associated with history of depression, prior psychiatric hospitalizations, and suicide attempts.

5. Take a thorough history of the client's suicidal thoughts and attempts, assessing the seriousness and lethality of these attempts.

6. Assess any history of the client's attempts at self-harm or parasuicidal behavior.

4. Describe dysfunctional family patterns of coping with stressors, and verbalize an understanding of how this has contributed to own current coping styles. (7)

7. Gather a complete family history of suicidal ideation and attempts, family history of depression, substance abuse, and other maladaptive means of coping with stress; compare and contrast this with the client's coping style.

5. Family and significant others provide information regarding the client's mental status. (8)

8. Meet with the family members to get collateral information about the client's emotional and behavioral status.

6. Accurately reveal current life stressors, strength of suicidal impulses, and ability to control those impulses. (9, 10, 11)

9. Encourage the client to identify current life stressors and their relationship to suicidal thinking and hopelessness.

10. Consider hospitalization by reviewing criteria for hospitalization with the client and hospital crisis worker (e.g., client feels unable to control suicidal impulses, attempt has occurred, lack of adequate support or supervision).

11. If the client meets legal criteria for involuntary commitment (e.g., high risk of being harmful to self) and refuses hospitalization, consult with other professionals regarding involuntary hospitalization, practicing acceptable standards of care throughout the assessment and treatment.

7. Cooperate with referral for hospitalization when recommended by therapist. (10, 11)

10. Consider hospitalization by reviewing criteria for hospitalization with the client and hospital crisis worker (e.g., client feels unable to control suicidal impulses, attempt has occurred, lack of adequate support or supervision).

11. If the client meets legal criteria for involuntary commitment (e.g., high risk of being harmful to self) and refuses hospitalization, consult with other professionals regarding involuntary hospitalization, practicing acceptable standards of care throughout the assessment and treatment.

8. Cooperate in constructing a safety plan and contracting for safety by signing written contract. (12, 13)

9. Verbalize an understanding of limits of confidentiality as applicable to suicide risk. (14, 15)

10. Report a decrease in the negative thinking that leads to hopelessness. (16, 17)

12. Outline and implement a short-term treatment plan to diminish or eliminate the immediacy of suicidal risk through eliminating access to lethal weapons or a large store of medication, and asking for the support and supervision of significant others.

13. Involve the family and the client's support group in safety, crisis, and hospital discharge plans, making sure that the family is capable of monitoring him/her if he/she is a minor.

14. Discuss issues of confidentiality with the client and the limits when it comes to suicidality, notifying him/her of a duty to report risk of self-harm to proper authorities.

15. Communicate the suicidal intent of the client to his/her parents, and work with them in constructing a safe home environment and 24-hour supervision of him/her.

16. Assist the client in identifying negative, distorted cognitive messages that lead to feeling hopeless and suicidal (e.g., "I'll never solve this problem"; "I'll never find another person to love me"; "nobody will ever forgive or respect me because I'm a totally bad person").

11. Identify feelings of guilt and shame that underline suicidal urges. (18, 19, 20)

12. Cooperate with a psychiatric evaluation for psychotropic medication. (21)

17. Teach the client positive, realistic self-talk that will lead to hope and acceptance (e.g., "I can learn problem-solving skills"; "there is more than one person in the world who can love me"; "I have made mistakes, but I do have good qualities and can be forgiven").

18. Explore the client's feelings of guilt and shame regarding the sexual abuse and how these feelings relate to suicidal thoughts. (See the Self-Blame chapter in the Victim Issues part of this Planner.)

19. Discuss with the sex abuse victim the irrational nature of feelings of guilt and shame; urge an attitude of empowerment that results from viewing himself/herself as a survivor. (See the Self-Blame chapter in the Victim Issues part of this Planner.)

20. Discuss the offender's feelings of shame and guilt within a context of need for treatment, reform, and forgiveness. (See the Self-Blame chapter in the Victim Issues part of this Planner.)

21. Refer the client to a psychiatrist to evaluate for the need for pharmacological intervention.

13. Take medication as prescribed, and report as to its side effects and effectiveness. (22)

14. Consent to a sharing of confidential information with an allied mental health professional in order to maximize the effectiveness of the treatment plan and to explore other treatment options. (23)

15. Verbalize a more realistic perspective about the source of suicidal urges. (24, 25, 26)

16. Identify successes from the past, and verbalize hope for the future. (27)

17. Make a written list of phone resources to be used during a crisis. (28, 29)

22. Monitor the client's medication compliance, effectiveness, and side effects; communicate this information to the prescribing physician.

23. After obtaining the client's signed permission, consult with other professionals regarding treatment decisions, referring the client for a second opinion regarding his/her treatment plan, if warranted.

24. Discuss with the client his/her ambivalent feelings about suicide and death.

25. Encourage the client to discuss his/her feelings of anger, rage, or retaliation and how turning these feelings inward can increase suicidality.

26. Assign the client journal writing to assist in identifying feelings and situations that intensify self-destructive urges.

27. Review the client's success that was attained in other difficult situations in the past, encouraging him/her to use those skills in present situations.

28. Ensure that the client is fully informed about crisis/24-hour availability of the clinician on call for emergencies.

29. Provide the client with evening and weekend crisis situation contact resources (e.g., therapist's 24-hour emergency services, local crisis/suicide hotlines, friends, family members, or local police).

18. Comply with the therapist's request for daily contact in order to assure safety during a crisis. (30, 31)

19. Follow through with professional recommendations for psychological testing. (32)

20. Report any changes in mood, suicidal urges, or feelings. (33, 34, 35)

21. Verbalize hope for the future and an improved mood. (36)

30. Monitor the client's mental status through daily telephone contact during times of crisis.

31. Intensify treatment during times of crisis by increasing the frequency of contacts with the client by daily office visits.

32. Refer the client for or administer psychological testing (e.g., Minnesota Multiphasic Personality Inventory, Rorschach Inkblot Test, Beck Depression Inventory).

33. Continue to evaluate the client periodically for suicide risk, especially during major life stressors, transitions, therapist absences/vacations, and so forth.

34. If the client becomes more depressed during the course of psychotherapy, perform a comprehensive reassessment; consider revision of treatment goals, intensi-fication of treatment, or referral for medication evaluation.

35. During a planned clinician absence, inform the clinician on call of the client's suicide risk, and communicate a contingency emergency plan.

36. Assist the client in identifying future experiences that he/she will enjoy, challenges that he/she will successfully meet, and responsibilities that he/she will capably fulfill.

__. _____   __. _____
     _____   _____

__. _____   __. _____
     _____   _____

__. _____   __. _____
     _____   _____

DIAGNOSTIC SUGGESTIONS:

ICD-9-CM	_ICD-10-CM_	_DSM-5_ Disorder, Condition, or Problem
296.xx	F32.x	Major Depressive Disorder, Single Episode
296.xx	F33.x	Major Depressive Disorder, Recurrent Episode
296.xx	F31.xx	Bipolar I Disorder
295.70	F25.0	Schizoaffective Disorder, Bipolar Type
295.70	F25.1	Schizoaffective Disorder, Depressive Type
309.81	F43.10	Posttraumatic Stress Disorder
301.83	F60.3	Borderline Personality Disorder
301.7	F60.2	Antisocial Personality Disorder
_____	_____	_____
_____	_____	_____

Appendix A

BIBLIOTHERAPY SUGGESTIONS

PART 1.   VICTIM ISSUES

Anger Difficulties

Ellis, A. (1977). *Anger: How to Live With and Without It.* Secaucus, NJ: Citadel Press.

Knopp, F. H. (1994). *When Your Wife Says No.* Brandon, VT.: Safer Society Press.

Lerner, H. (1985). *The Dance of Anger: A Woman's Guide to Changing the Patterns of Intimate Relationships.* New York: Harper Perennial.

McKay, M., P. Rogers, and J. McKay (1989). *When Anger Hurts.* Oakland, CA: New Harbinger.

Rosellini, G., and M. Worden (1986). *Of Course You're Angry.* San Francisco: Harper Hazelden.

Rubin, T. I. (1969). *The Angry Book.* New York: Macmillan.

Tavris, C. (1989). *Anger: The Misunderstood Emotion.* New York: Touchstone Books.

Weisinger, H. (1985). *Dr. Weisinger's Anger Work Out Book.* New York: Quill.

Dissociation

Bass, E., and L. Davis (1988). *The Courage to Heal: A Guide for Women Survivors of Child Sexual Abuse.* San Francisco: HarperCollins.

Cohen, B. M., E. Giller, and Lynn W. _____ (client) (eds.) (1991). *Multiple Personality Disorder from the Inside Out.* Towson, MD: Sidron Press.

Grateful Members of Emotional Health Anonymous (1982). *The Twelve Steps for Everyone . . . Who Really Wants Them.* Minneapolis, MN: CompCare.

Eating Disorders

Burns, D. (1993). *Ten Days to Self-Esteem!* New York: William Morrow.

Fairburn, C. (1995). *Overcoming Binge Eating.* New York: Guilford.

Hirschmann, J., and C. Munter (1988). *Overcoming Overeating.* New York: Ballantine Books.

Hollis, J. (1985). *Fat Is a Family Affair.* New York: Harper & Row.

Rodin, J. (1993). *Body Traps.* New York: William Morrow.

Roth, G. (2002). *Feeding the Hungry Heart: The Experience of Compulsive Eating.* New York: Macmillan.

Sacker, I., and M. Zimmer (1987). *Dying to Be Thin.* New York: Warner Books.

Shapiro, L. (1993). *Building Blocks of Self Esteem.* King of Prussia, PA: Center for Applied Psychology.

Siegel, M., J. Brisman, and M. Weinshel (1997). *Surviving an Eating Disorder.* San Francisco: HarperCollins.

Emotional Dysregulation

Ainscough, C., and K. Toon (2000). *Surviving Childhood Sexual Abuse Workbook.* Tucson, AZ.: Fisher Books.

Cudney, M., and R. Handy (1993). *Self-Defeating Behaviors.* San Francisco: Harper-Collins.

Katherine, A. (1991). *Boundaries: Where You End and I Begin.* New York: Simon & Schuster.

Katherine, A. (2000). *Where to Draw the Line: How to Set Healthy Boundaries Every Day.* New York: Simon & Schuster.

Peurito, R. (1997). *Overcoming Anxiety.* New York: Henry Holt.

Moskovitz, R. A. (2001). *Lost in the Mirror: An Inside Look at Borderline Personality Disorder.* Dallas, TX: Taylor Publishing.

Santoro, J., and R. Cohen (1997). *The Angry Heart: Overcoming Borderline and Addictive Disorders: An Interactive Self-Help Guide.* Oakland, CA: New Harbinger.

Posttraumatic Stress Disorder (PTSD)

Ainscough, C., and K. Toon (2000). *Surviving Childhood Sexual Abuse Workbook.* Tucson, AZ.: Fisher Books.

Jeffers, S. (1987). *Feel the Fear and Do It Anyway.* New York: Random House.

Kushner, H. (1981). *When Bad Things Happen to Good People.* New York: Schocken Books.

Leith, L. (1998). *Exercising Your Way to Better Mental Health.* Morgantown, WV: Fitness Information Technology.

Matsakis, A. (1992). *I Can't Get Over It: A Handbook for Trauma Survivors.* Oakland, CA: New Harbinger.

Simon, S., and S. Simon (1990). *Forgiving: How to Make Peace with Your Past and Get On with Your Life.* New York: Warner Books.

Walker, A. (1996). *The Color Purple.* New York: Pocket Books.

Self-Blame

Ainscough, C., and K. Toon (2000). *Surviving Childhood Sexual Abuse: Revised Edition.* Tucson, AZ: Fisher Books.

Bass, E., and L. Davis (1988). *The Courage to Heal: A Guide for Women Survivors of Child Sexual Abuse.* San Francisco: HarperCollins.

Bradshaw, J. (1988). *Healing the Shame That Binds You.* Deerfield Beach, FL: Health Communications.

Burns, D. (1980). *Feeling Good: The New Mood Therapy.* New York: Signet.

Burns, D. (1993). *Ten Days to Self Esteem!* New York: William Morrow.

Davis, L. (1990). *The Courage to Heal Workbook: For Men and Women Survivors of Child Sexual Abuse.* San Francisco: HarperCollins.

Forward, S., and C. Buck (1978). *Betrayal of Innocence: Incest and Its Devastation.* New York: Penguin Books.

Fossum, M. A., and M. J. Mason (1986). *Facing Shame: Families in Recovery.* New York: Norton.

Gil, E. (1984). *Outgrowing the Pain: A Book for and About Adults Abused as Children.* New York: Dell Publishing.

Kaufman, G. (1992). *Shame: The Power of Caring.* Rochester, VT: Schenkman Books.

Kubler-Ross, E. (1997). *On Death and Dying.* New York: Scribner.

Kushner, H. (1981). *When Bad Things Happen to Good People.* New York: Schocken Books.

Lew, M., and E. Bass (2000). *Victims No Longer: Men Recovering From Incest and Other Sexual Child Abuse.* New York: HarperCollins.

Simon, S., and S. Simon (1990). *Forgiving: How to Make Peace with Your Past and Get On with Your Life.* New York: Warner Books.

Smedes, L. (1991). *Forgive and Forget: Healing the Hurts We Don't Deserve.* San Francisco: Harper.

Walker, A. (1996). *The Color Purple.* New York: Pocket Books.

Westberg, G. (1986). *Good Grief.* Philadelphia: Fortress Press.

Whitfield, C. (1987). *Healing the Child Within.* Deerfield Beach, FL: Health Communications.

Whitfield, C. (1990). *A Gift To Myself.* Deerfield Beach, FL: Health Communications.

Self-Injury

Contario, K., W. Lader, and J. Kingson (1999). *Bodily Harm: The Breakthrough Healing Program for Self-Injurers.* New York: Hyperion.

Miller, D. (1995) *Women Who Hurt Themselves: A Book of Hope and Understanding.* New York: Basic Books.

Trautman, K., and R. Connors (1994). *Understanding Self-Injury: A Workbook for Adults.* Pittsburgh, PA: Pittsburgh Action Against Rape.

Social Withdrawal

Barlow, D. H., and M. G. Craske (1989). *Mastery of Your Anxiety and Panic.* Albany, NY: Graywind Publications.

Bass, E., and L. Davis (1988). *The Courage to Heal: A Guide for Women Survivors of Child Sexual Abuse.* San Francisco: HarperCollins.

Bradshaw, J. (1988). *Healing the Shame That Binds You.* Deerfield Beach, FL: Health Communications.

Burns, D. (1985). *Intimate Connections: The New Clinically Tested Program for Overcoming Loneliness.* New York: William Morrow.

Burns, D. (1993). *Ten Days to Self Esteem!* New York: William Morrow.

Carmin, C. N., C. A. Pollard, T. Flynn, and B. G. Morkway. *Dying of Embarrassment: Help for Social Anxiety and Phobia.* Oakland, CA: New Harbinger Press.

Dyer, W. (1978). *Pulling Your Own Strings.* New York: T. Crowell.

Fossum, M. A., and M. J. Mason (1986). *Facing Shame: Families in Recovery.* New York: Norton.

Harris, A., and T. Harris (1969). *I'm OK You're OK.* New York: Harper & Row.

James, M., and D. Jongeward (1971). *Born to Win.* Reading, MA: Addison-Wesley.

Nouwen, H. (1975). *Reaching Out.* New York: Doubleday.

Zimbardo, P. (1987). *Shyness: What It Is and What to Do About It.* Reading, MA: Addison-Wesley.

Trust Impairment

Abrahms-Spring, J. (1996). *After the Affair.* New York: Harper Collins.

Bach, G., and P. Wyden (1976). *The Intimate Enemy: How to Fight Fair in Love and Marriage.* New York: Avon Books.

Bradshaw, J. (1988). *Healing the Shame That Binds You.* Deerfield Beach, FL: Health Communications.

Colgrove, M., H. Bloomfield, and P. McWilliams (1991). *How to Survive the Loss of a Love.* Los Angeles: Prelude Press.

Fisher, B. (1981). *Rebuilding: When Your Relationship Ends.* San Luis Obispo, CA: Impact.

Fossum, M. A., and M. J. Mason (1986). *Facing Shame: Families in Recovery.* New York: Norton.

Fromm, E. (1956). *The Art of Loving.* New York: Harper & Row.

Gorski, T. (1993). *Getting Love Right: Learning the Choices of Healthy Intimacy.* New York: Simon & Schuster.

Gray, J. (1992). *Men Are from Mars, Women Are from Venus.* New York: HarperCollins.

Gray, J. (1993). *Men and Women and Relationships: Making Peace with the Opposite Sex.* Hillsboro, OR: Beyond Words.

Harley, W. (1994). *His Needs, Her Needs: Building an Affair-Proof Marriage.* Grand Rapids, MI: Revell.

Hendrix, H. (1988). *Getting the Love You Want.* New York: Henry Holt.

Lerner, H. (1989). *The Dance of Intimacy: A Woman's Guide to Courageous Acts of Change in Key Relationships.* New York: Harper Perennial.

Markman, H., S. Stanley, and S. Blumberg (1994). *Fighting for Your Marriage*. San Francisco: Jossey-Bass.

Schnarch, D. (1997). *Passionate Marriage*. New York: Norton.

Subotnik, R., and G. Harris (1994). *Surviving Infidelity*. Holbrook, MA: Bob Adams.

Walker, A. (1996). *The Color Purple*. New York: Pocket Books.

PART 2.   OFFENDER ISSUES

Anger Difficulties

Ellis, A. (1977). *Anger: How to Live With and Without It*. Secaucus, NJ: Citadel Press.

Knopp, F. H. (1994). *When Your Wife Says No*. Brandon, VT.: Safer Society Press.

Lerner, H. (1985). *The Dance of Anger: A Woman's Guide to Changing the Patterns of Intimate Relationships*. New York: Harper Perennial.

McKay, M., P. Rogers, and J. McKay (1989). *When Anger Hurts*. Oakland, CA: New Harbinger.

Rosellini, G., and M. Worden (1986). *Of Course You're Angry*. San Francisco: Harper Hazelden.

Rubin, T. I. (1969). *The Angry Book*. New York: Macmillan.

Tavris, C. (1989). *Anger: The Misunderstood Emotion*. New York: Touchstone Books.

Weisinger, H. (1985). *Dr. Weisinger's Anger Work Out Book*. New York: Quill.

Cleric Offender

Cleaver, E. (1992). *The Soul on Fire*. Grand Rapids, MI: Zondervan.

Foster, R. (1978). *Celebration of Discipline*. New York: Harper & Row.

Helmfelt, R., and R. Fowler (1990). *Serenity: A Companion for 12 Step Recovery*. Nashville, TN: Nelson.

Horton, T. (2002). *Walk the Walk: A Treatment Supplement for Sex Offenders with Christian Beliefs*. Peoria, IL: Tim Horton.

Laaser, M. (1996). *Restoring the Soul of a Church: Reconciling Congregations Wounded by Clergy Sexual Misconduct*. Collegeville, MN: Liturgical Press.

Miles, J. (1995). *God: A Biography*. New York: Alfred Knopf.

Moore, T. (1992). *Care of the Soul*. New York: HarperCollins.

Norris, K. (1996). *The Cloister Walk*. New York: Riverhead Books.

Peck, M. S. (1978). *The Road Less Traveled*. New York: Simon & Schuster.

Peck, M. S. (1993). *Further Along the Road Less Traveled*. New York: Simon & Schuster.

Presnall, L. (1959). *Search for Serenity: And How to Achieve It*. Salt Lake City, UT: V.A.F. Publishing.

Rossetti, S. J. (1996). *A Tragic Grace: The Catholic Church and Child Sexual Abuse*. Collegeville, MN: Liturgical Press.

Schaumburg, H. W. (1997). *False Intimacy: Understanding the Struggle of Sexual Addiction*. Colorado Springs, CO: NavPress.

Cognitive Distortions

Bays, L., and R. Freeman-Longo (1989). *Why Did I Do It Again? Understanding My Cycle of Problem Behaviors.* Orwell, VT: Safer Society Press.
Bays, L., and R. Freeman-Longo (1990) *How Can I Stop? Breaking My Deviant Cycle.* Orwell, VT: Safer Society Press.
Freeman-Longo, R., and L. Bays (1988). *Who Am I and Why Am I in Treatment?* Orwell, VT: Safer Society Press.
Freeman-Longo, R., L. Bays, and E. Bear (1995). *Empathy and Compassionate Action: Issues and Exercises: A Workbook for Clients in Treatment.* Brandon, VT: Safer Society Press.
Scieszka, J., and L. Smith (1989) *The True Story of the 3 Little Pigs! By A. Wolf.* New York: Puffin Books.
Steen, C. (1993). *The Relapse Prevention Workbook for Youth in Treatment.* Brandon, VT: Safer Society Press.
Steen, C. (2001). *The Adult Relapse Prevention Workbook.* Brandon, VT: Sager Society Press.

Denial

Bays, L., and R. Freeman-Longo (1990) *How Can I Stop? Breaking My Deviant Cycle.* Orwell, VT: Safer Society Press.
Freeman-Longo, R., and L. Bays (1988). *Who Am I and Why Am I in Treatment?* Orwell, VT: Safer Society Press.
Freeman-Longo, R., L. Bays, and E. Bear (1995). *Empathy and Compassionate Action: Issues and Exercises: A Workbook for Clients in Treatment.* Brandon, VT: Safer Society Press.
Scieszka, J., and L. Smith (1989). *The True Story of the 3 Little Pigs! By A. Wolf.* New York: Puffin Books.
Steen, C. (1993). *The Relapse Prevention Workbook for Youth in Treatment.* Brandon, VT: Safer Society Press.
Steen, C. (2001). *The Adult Relapse Prevention Workbook.* Brandon, VT: Sager Society Press.

Deviant Sexual Arousal

Bays, L., and R. Freeman-Longo (1989). *Why Did I Do It Again? Understanding My Cycle of Problem Behaviors.* Orwell, VT: Safer Society Press.
Bays, L., and R. Freeman-Longo (1990) *How Can I Stop? Breaking My Deviant Cycle.* Orwell, VT: Safer Society Press.
Freeman-Longo, R., and L. Bays (1988). *Who Am I and Why Am I in Treatment?* Orwell, VT: Safer Society Press.
Freeman-Longo, R., L. Bays, and E. Bear (1995). *Empathy and Compassionate Action: Issues and Exercises: A Workbook for Clients in Treatment.* Brandon, VT: Safer Society Press.

Scieszka, J., and L. Smith (1989). *The True Story of the 3 Little Pigs! By A. Wolf.* New York: Puffin Books.

Steen, C. (1993). *The Relapse Prevention Workbook for Youth in Treatment.* Brandon, VT: Safer Society Press.

Steen, C. (2001). *The Adult Relapse Prevention Workbook.* Brandon, VT: Sager Society Press.

Empathy Deficits

Bays, L., and R. Freeman-Longo (1989). *Why Did I Do It Again? Understanding My Cycle of Problem Behaviors.* Orwell, VT: Safer Society Press.

Bays, L., and R. Freeman-Longo (1990). *How Can I Stop? Breaking My Deviant Cycle.* Orwell, VT: Safer Society Press.

Freeman-Longo, R., and L. Bays (1988). *Who Am I and Why Am I in Treatment?* Orwell, VT: Safer Society Press.

Freeman-Longo, R., L. Bays, and E. Bear (1995). *Empathy and Compassionate Action: Issues and Exercises: A Workbook for Clients in Treatment.* Brandon, VT: Safer Society Press.

Steen, C. (1993). *The Relapse Prevention Workbook for Youth in Treatment.* Brandon, VT: Safer Society Press.

Steen, C. (2001). *The Adult Relapse Prevention Workbook.* Brandon, VT: Sager Society Press.

Female Offender

Hendrix, H. (1988). *Getting the Love You Want: A Guide for Couples.* New York: Henry Holt.

Hyde, J., and J. DeLamater (1999). *Understanding Human Sexuality.* New York: McGraw-Hill.

Katherine, A. (1991). *Boundaries: Where You End and I Begin.* New York: Fireside.

Smith, M. J. (1985). *When I Say No I Feel Guilty.* New York: Bantam Books.

Steen, C. (2001). *The Adult Relapse Prevention Workbook.* Brandon, VT: Sager Society Press.

Zoldbrod, A. (1998). *Sex Smart: How Your Childhood Shaped Your Sexual Life and What to Do About It.* Oakland, CA: New Harbinger Publications.

Guilt/Shame

Bradshaw, J. (1988). *Healing the Shame That Binds You.* Deer Field Beach, FL: Health Communication.

Burns, D. (1980). *Feeling Good: The New Mood Therapy.* New York: Cignet.

Burns, D. (1990). *The Feeling Good Handbook.* New York: Plume.

Fossum, M., and M. Mason (1989). *Facing Shame.* New York: W.W. Norton & Co.

Helmstetter, S. (1997). *What to Say When You Talk to Yourself.* New York: Fine Communications.

Simon, S., and S. Simon (1990). *Forgiving: How to Make Peace with Your Past and Get On with Your Life.* New York: Warner Books.

Legal Issues

Carnes, P. (1983). *Out of the Shadows: Understanding Sexual Addictions.* Minneapolis, MN: CompCare.

Williams, R., and Williams, V. (1993). *Anger Kills.* New York: Time Books.

Relapse Prevention

Bays, L., and R. Freeman-Longo (1989). *Why Did I Do It Again? Understanding My Cycle of Problem Behaviors.* Orwell, VT: Safer Society Press.

Bays, L., and R. Freeman-Longo (1990). *How Can I Stop? Breaking My Deviant Cycle.* Orwell, VT: Safer Society Press.

Freeman-Longo, R., and L. Bays (1988). *Who Am I and Why Am I in Treatment?* Orwell, VT: Safer Society Press.

Freeman-Longo, R., L. Bays, and E. Bear (1995). *Empathy and Compassionate Action: Issues and Exercises: A Workbook for Clients in Treatment.* Brandon, VT: Safer Society Press.

Scieszka, J., and L. Smith (1989). *The True Story of the 3 Little Pigs! By A. Wolf.* New York: Puffin Books.

Steen, C. (1993). *The Relapse Prevention Workbook for Youth in Treatment.* Brandon, VT: Safer Society Press.

Steen, C. (2001). *The Adult Relapse Prevention Workbook.* Brandon, VT: Safer Society Press.

Relationship Skills Deficits

Abrahms-Spring, J. (1996). *After the Affair.* New York: Harper Collins.

Bach, G., and P. Wyden (1976). *The Intimate Enemy: How to Fight Fair in Love and Marriage.* New York: Avon Books.

Colgrove, M., H. Bloomfield, and P. McWilliams (1991). *How to Survive the Loss of a Love.* Los Angeles: Prelude Press.

Fisher, B. (1981). *ReBuilding: When Your Relationship Ends.* San Luis Obispo, CA: Impact.

Fromm, E. (1956). *The Art of Loving.* New York: Harper & Row.

Gorski, T. (1993). *Getting Love Right: Learning the Choices of Healthy Intimacy.* New York: Simon & Schuster.

Gray, J. (1992). *Men Are from Mars, Women Are from Venus.* New York: Harper-Collins.

Gray, J. (1993). *Men and Women and Relationships: Making Peace with the Opposite Sex.* Hillsboro, OR: Beyond Words.

Harley, W. (1994). *His Needs, Her Needs: Building an Affair-Proof Marriage.* Grand Rapids, MI: Revell.

Hendrix, H. (1988). *Getting the Love You Want.* New York: Henry Holt.

Lerner, H. (1989). *The Dance of Intimacy: A Woman's Guide to Courageous Acts of Change in Key Relationships.* New York: Harper Perennial.

Lindbergh, A. (1955). *A Gift from the Sea.* New York: Pantheon.

Markman, H., S. Stanley, and S. Blumberg (1994). *Fighting for Your Marriage.* San Francisco: Jossey-Bass.

Steen, C. (2001). *The Adult Relapse Prevention Workbook.* Brandon, VT: Sager Society Press.

PART 3.   OFFENDER AND VICTIM ISSUES

Anxiety, Panic, and Depression

Barlow, D. H., and M. G. Craske (1989). *Mastery of Your Anxiety and Panic.* Albany, NY: Graywind Publications.

Benson, H. (1975). *The Relaxation Response.* New York: William Morrow.

Burns, D. (1980). *Feeling Good: The New Mood Therapy.* New York: Signet.

Burns, D. (1989). *The Feeling Good Handbook.* New York: Plume.

Burns, D. (1993). *Ten Days to Self-Esteem!* New York: William Morrow.

Butler, P. (1991). *Talking to Yourself: Learning the Language of Self-Affirmation.* New York: Stein and Day.

Davis, M., E. Eshelman, and M. McKay (2000). *The Relaxation and Stress Reduction Workbook.* Oakland, CA: New Harbinger.

Gold, M. (1988). *The Good News About Panic, Anxiety, and Phobias.* New York: Villard/Random House.

Hauck, P. (1975). *Overcoming Worry and Fear.* Philadelphia, PA: Westminster Press.

Jeffers, S. (1987). *Feel the Fear and Do It Anyway.* San Diego, CA: Harcourt Brace Jovanovich.

Leith, L. (1998). *Exercising Your Way to Better Mental Health.* Morgantown, WV: Fitness Information Technology.

Marks, I. (1980). *Living with Fear: Understanding and Coping with Anxiety.* New York: McGraw-Hill.

Swede, S., and S. Jaffe (1987). *The Panic Attack Recovery Book.* New York: New American Library.

Wilson, R. (1986). *Don't Panic: Taking Control of Anxiety Attacks.* New York: Harper & Row.

Zonnebelt-Smeenge, S., and R. DeVries (1998). *Getting to the Other Side of Grief: Overcoming the Loss of a Spouse.* Grand Rapids, MI: Baker.

Family Reunification

Levenson, J. S., and J. W. Morin (2001). *Connections Workbook*. Thousand Oaks, CA: Sage.

Self-Esteem Deficit

Branden, N. (1994). *The Six Pillars of Self-Esteem*. New York: Bantam Books.

Burns, D. (1993). *Ten Days to Self Esteem!* New York: William Morrow.

Davis, M., E. Eshelman, and M. McKay (2000). *The Relaxation and Stress Reduction Workbook*. Oakland, CA: New Harbinger.

Helmstetter, S. (1986). *What to Say When You Talk to Yourself.* New York: Fine Communications.

McKay, M., and P. Fanning (1987). *Self-Esteem*. Oakland, CA: New Harbinger.

Shapiro, L. (1993). *Building Blocks of Self Esteem*. King of Prussia, PA: Center for Applied Psychology.

Zimbardo, P. (1987). *Shyness: What It Is and What to Do About It*. Reading, MA: Addison-Wesley.

Sexual Dysfunction

Abrahms-Spring, J. (1996). *After the Affair*. New York: Harper Collins.

Barbach, L. (1982). *For Each Other: Sharing Sexual Intimacy*. New York: Doubleday.

Block, J. D. (1991). *Sex Over 50*. Paramus, NJ: Reward Books.

Carnes, P. (1983). *Out of the Shadows: Understanding Sexual Addictions*. Minneapolis, MN: CompCare.

Carnes, P. (1991). *Don't Call It Love: Recovery from Sexual Addiction*. Phoenix, AZ: Gentle Path Press.

Carnes, P. J. (1997). *Sexual Anorexia: Overcoming Sexual Self-Hatred*. Center City, MN: Hazelden.

Carnes, P., D. Delmonico, E. Griffin, and J. Moriarity (2001). *In the Shadows of the Net: Breaking Free of Compulsive Online Sexual Behavior*. Center City, MN.: Hazelden.

Comfort, A. (1991). *The New Joy of Sex*. New York: Crown.

Delmonico, D. L., E. Griffin, and J. Moriarity (2001). *Cybersex Unhooked: A Workbook for Breaking Free of Compulsive Online Sexual Behavior*. Wickenburg, AZ.: Gentle Path Press.

Haines, S. (1999). *The Survivor's Guide to Sex*. San Francisco: Cleis Press.

Heiman, J., and J. LoPiccolo (1988). *Becoming Orgasmic: A Sexual Growth Program for Women*. New York: Prentice-Hall.

Knopf, J., and M. Seiler (1990). *Inhibited Sexual Desire*. New York: Warner Books.

McCarthy, B., and E. McCarthy (1984). *Sexual Awareness*. New York: Carroll & Graf.

Penner, C., and C. Penner (1981). *The Gift of Sex*. Waco, TX: Word.

Schaumburg, H. W. (1997). *False Intimacy: Understanding the Struggle of Sexual Addiction.* Colorado Springs, CO: NavPress.

Subotnik, R., and G. Harris (1994). *Surviving Infidelity.* Holbrook, MA: Bob Adams.

Valins, L. (1992). *When a Woman's Body Says No to Sex: Understanding and Overcoming Vaginismus.* New York: Penguin.

Westheimer, R. (2000). *Sex for Dummies: A Reference for the Rest of Us.* Hoboken, NJ: John Wiley & Sons.

Zilbergeld, B. (1992). *The New Male Sexuality.* New York: Bantam.

Stress Management Deficits

Davis, M., E. Eshelman, and M. McKay (2000). *The Relaxation and Stress Reduction Workbook.* Oakland, CA: New Harbinger.

Friedman, M., and D. Olmer (1984). *Treating Type A Behaviors and Your Heart.* New York: Alfred Knopf.

Glasser, W. (1976). *Positive Addiction.* San Francisco: HarperCollins.

Kirsta, A. (1987). *The Book of Stress Survival: Identifying and Reducing the Stress in Your Life.* New York: Fireside Press.

Peck, M. S. (1978). *The Road Less Traveled.* New York: Simon & Schuster.

Peck, M. S. (1993). *Further Along the Road Less Traveled.* New York: Simon & Schuster.

Pirsig, R. (1974). *Zen and the Art of Motorcycle Maintenance.* New York: William Morrow.

Robinson, B. (1993). *Overdoing It.* Deerfield Beach, FL: Health Communications.

Substance Abuse

Alcoholics Anonymous (1975). *Living Sober.* New York: A.A. World Service.

Alcoholics Anonymous (1976). *Alcoholics Anonymous: The Big Book.* New York: A.A. World Service.

Carnes, P. (1989). *A Gentle Path Through the Twelve Steps.* Minneapolis, MN: CompCare.

Drews, T. R. (1980). *Getting Them Sober: A Guide for Those Living with Alcoholism.* South Plainfield, NJ: Bridge Publishing.

Gorski, T. (1989–92). *The Staying Sober Workbook.* Independence, MO: Herald House Press.

Gorski, T., and M. Miller (1986). *Staying Sober: A Guide to Relapse Prevention.* Independence, MO: Herald House Press.

Johnson, V. (1980). *I'll Quit Tomorrow.* New York: Harper & Row.

Kasl-Davis, C. (1992). *Many Roads, One Journey.* New York: HarperCollins.

Larson, E. (1985). *Stage II Recovery: Life Beyond Addiction.* San Francisco: Harper & Row.

Nuckals, C. (1989). *Cocaine: From Dependence to Recovery.* Blue Ridge Summit, PA: TAB Books.

Wilson, B. (1967). *As Bill Sees It.* New York: A.A. World Service.

Suicidal Ideation/Attempt

Butler, P. (1991). *Talking to Yourself: Learning the Language of Self-Affirmation.* New York: Stein and Day.

Hutschnecker, A. (1951). *The Will to Live.* New York: Cornerstone Library.

Seligman, M. (1990). *Learned Optimism: The Skill to Conquer Life's Obstacles, Large and Small.* New York: Pocket Books.

Appendix B

RECOVERY MODEL OBJECTIVES AND INTERVENTIONS

The Objectives and Interventions that follow are created around the 10 core principles developed by a multidisciplinary panel at the 2004 National Consensus Conference on Mental Health Recovery and Mental Health Systems Transformation, convened by the Substance Abuse and Mental Health Services Administration (SAMHSA, 2004):

1. **Self-direction:** Consumers lead, control, exercise choice over, and determine their own path of recovery by optimizing autonomy, independence, and control of resources to achieve a self-determined life. By definition, the recovery process must be self-directed by the individual, who defines his or her own life goals and designs a unique path toward those goals.
2. **Individualized and person-centered:** There are multiple pathways to recovery based on an individual's unique strengths and resiliencies as well as his or her needs, preferences, experiences (including past trauma), and cultural background in all of its diverse representations. Individuals also identify recovery as being an ongoing journey and an end result as well as an overall paradigm for achieving wellness and optimal mental health.
3. **Empowerment:** Consumers have the authority to choose from a range of options and to participate in all decisions—including the allocation of resources—that will affect their lives, and are educated and supported in so doing. They have the ability to join with other consumers to collectively and effectively speak for themselves about their needs, wants, desires, and aspirations. Through empowerment, an individual gains control of his or her own destiny and influences the organizational and societal structures in his or her life.
4. **Holistic:** Recovery encompasses an individual's whole life, including mind, body, spirit, and community. Recovery embraces all aspects of life, including housing, employment, education, mental health and healthcare treatment and services, complementary and naturalistic services, addictions treatment, spirituality, creativity, social networks, community participation, and family supports as determined by the person. Families,

providers, organizations, systems, communities, and society play crucial roles in creating and maintaining meaningful opportunities for consumer access to these supports.

5. **Nonlinear:** Recovery is not a step-by-step process but one based on continual growth, occasional setbacks, and learning from experience. Recovery begins with an initial stage of awareness in which a person recognizes that positive change is possible. This awareness enables the consumer to move on to fully engage in the work of recovery.

6. **Strengths-based:** Recovery focuses on valuing and building on the multiple capacities, resiliencies, talents, coping abilities, and inherent worth of individuals. By building on these strengths, consumers leave stymied life roles behind and engage in new life roles (e.g., partner, caregiver, friend, student, employee). The process of recovery moves forward through interaction with others in supportive, trust-based relationships.

7. **Peer support:** Mutual support—including the sharing of experiential knowledge and skills and social learning—plays an invaluable role in recovery. Consumers encourage and engage other consumers in recovery and provide each other with a sense of belonging, supportive relationships, valued roles, and community.

8. **Respect:** Community, systems, and societal acceptance and appreciation of consumers—including protecting their rights and eliminating discrimination and stigma—are crucial in achieving recovery. Self-acceptance and regaining belief in one's self are particularly vital. Respect ensures the inclusion and full participation of consumers in all aspects of their lives.

9. **Responsibility:** Consumers have a personal responsibility for their own self-care and journeys of recovery. Taking steps toward their goals may require great courage. Consumers must strive to understand and give meaning to their experiences and identify coping strategies and healing processes to promote their own wellness.

10. **Hope:** Recovery provides the essential and motivating message of a better future—that people can overcome the barriers and obstacles that confront them. Hope is internalized, but can be fostered by peers, families, friends, providers, and others. Hope is the catalyst of the recovery process. Mental health recovery not only benefits individuals with mental health disabilities by focusing on their abilities to live, work, learn, and fully participate in our society, but also enriches the texture of American community life. America reaps the benefits of the contributions individuals with mental disabilities can make, ultimately becoming a stronger and healthier Nation.[1]

---

[1]From: Substance Abuse and Mental Health Services Administration's (SAMHSA) National Mental Health Information Center: Center for Mental Health Services (2004). *National consensus statement on mental health recovery.* Washington, DC: Author. Available from http://mentalhealth.samhsa.gov/publications/allpubs/sma05-4129/

The numbers used for Objectives in the treatment plan that follows correspond to the numbers for the 10 core principles. Each of the 10 Objectives was written to capture the essential theme of the like-numbered core principle. The numbers in parentheses after the Objectives denote the Interventions designed to assist the client in attaining each respective Objective. The clinician may select any or all of the Objectives and Intervention statements to include in the client's treatment plan.

One generic Long-Term Goal statement is offered should the clinician desire to emphasize a recovery model orientation in the client's treatment plan.

LONG-TERM GOAL

1. To live a meaningful life in a self-selected community while striving to achieve full potential during the journey of healing and transformation.

SHORT-TERM OBJECTIVES

1. Make it clear to therapist, family, and friends what path to recovery is preferred. (1, 2, 3, 4)

THERAPEUTIC INTERVENTIONS

1. Explore the client's thoughts, needs, and preferences regarding his/her desired pathway to recovery (from depression, bipolar disorder, posttraumatic stress disorder [PTSD], etc.).

2. Discuss with the client the alternative treatment interventions and community support resources that might facilitate his/her recovery.

3. Solicit from the client his/her preferences regarding the direction treatment will take; allow for these preferences to be communicated to family and significant others.

4. Discuss and process with the client the possible outcomes that may result from his/her decisions.

2. Specify any unique needs and cultural preferences that must be taken under consideration during the treatment process. (5, 6)

3. Verbalize an understanding that decision making throughout the treatment process is self-controlled. (7, 8)

4. Express mental, physical, spiritual, and community needs and desires that should be integrated into the treatment process. (9, 10)

5. Verbalize an understanding that during the treatment process there will be successes and failures, progress and setbacks. (11, 12)

5. Explore with the client any cultural considerations, experiences, or other needs that must be considered in formulating a mutually agreed-upon treatment plan.

6. Modify treatment planning to accommodate the client's cultural and experiential background and preferences.

7. Clarify with the client that he/she has the right to choose and select among options and participate in all decisions that affect him/her during treatment.

8. Continuously offer and explain options to the client as treatment progresses in support of his/her sense of empowerment, encouraging and reinforcing the client's participation in treatment decision making.

9. Assess the client's personal, interpersonal, medical, spiritual, and community strengths and weaknesses.

10. Maintain a holistic approach to treatment planning by integrating the client's unique mental, physical, spiritual, and community needs and assets into the plan; arrive at an agreement with the client as to how these integrations will be made.

11. Facilitate realistic expectations and hope in the client that positive change is possible, but

does not occur in a linear process of straight-line successes; emphasize a recovery process involving growth, learning from advances as well as setbacks, and staying this course toward recovery.

12. Convey to the client that you will stay the course with him/her through the difficult times of lapses and setbacks.

6. Cooperate with an assessment of personal strengths and assets brought to the treatment process. (13, 14, 15)

13. Administer to the client the *Behavioral and Emotional Rating Scale (BERS): A Strength-Based Approach to Assessment* (Epstein).

14. Identify the client's strengths through a thorough assessment involving social, cognitive, relational, and spiritual aspects of the client's life; assist the client in identifying what coping skills have worked well in the past to overcome problems and what talents and abilities characterize his/her daily life.

15. Provide feedback to the client of his/her identified strengths and how these strengths can be integrated into short-term and long-term recovery planning.

7. Verbalize an understanding of the benefits of peer support during the recovery process. (16, 17, 18)

16. Discuss with the client the benefits of peer support (e.g., sharing common problems, receiving advice regarding successful coping skills, getting encouragement, learning of helpful community

resources, etc.) toward the client's agreement to engage in peer activity.

17. Refer the client to peer support groups of his/her choice in the community and process his/her experience with follow-through.

18. Build and reinforce the client's sense of belonging, supportive relationship building, social value, and community integration by processing the gains and problem-solving the obstacles encountered through the client's social activities.

8. Agree to reveal when any occasion arises that respect is not felt from the treatment staff, family, self, or the community. (19, 20, 21)

19. Discuss with the client the crucial role that respect plays in recovery, reviewing subtle and obvious ways in which disrespect may be shown to or experienced by the client.

20. Review ways in which the client has felt disrespected in the past, identifying sources of that disrespect.

21. Encourage and reinforce the client's self-concept as a person deserving of respect; advocate for the client to increase incidents of respectful treatment within the community and/or family system.

9. Verbalize acceptance of responsibility for self-care and participation in decisions during the treatment process. (22)

22. Develop, encourage, support, and reinforce the client's role as the person in control of his/her treatment and responsible for its application to his/her daily life; adopt a supportive role as a resource

person to assist in the recovery process.

10. Express hope that better functioning in the future can be attained. (23, 24)

23. Discuss with the client potential role models who have achieved a more satisfying life by using their personal strengths, skills, and social support to live, work, learn, and fully participate in society toward building hope and incentive motivation.

24. Discuss and enhance internalization of the client's self-concept as a person capable of overcoming obstacles and achieving satisfaction in living; continuously build and reinforce this self-concept using past and present examples supporting it.